ENTERPRISE
INTEGRATION

Kent Sandoe
Gail Corbitt
Raymond Boykin

California State University, Chico

with contributions by
James Connolly and Aditya Saharia

JOHN WILEY & SONS, INC.

NEW YORK • CHICHESTER • WEINHEIM • BRISBANE • SINGAPORE • TORONTO

ACQUISITIONS EDITOR	Beth L. Golub
MARKETING MANAGER	Jessica Garcia
SENIOR PRODUCTION EDITOR	Christine Cervoni
COVER DESIGNER	Maddy Lesure
FRONT COVER ILLUSTRATION	Gert Jan Hofstede

To order books or for customer service call 1-800-CALL-WILEY (225-5945)

Library of Congress Cataloging-in-Publication Data

Sandoe, Kent
   Enterprise Integration / Kent Sandoe, Gail Corbitt, Raymond Boykin
      p. cm.
   Includes index.
   ISBN 0-471-35993-9 (Cloth : alk. paper)
      1. Management information systems. 2. Information resources management. I. Title.

T58.6 .S265 2001
658'.05--dc21   2001017665

10 9 8 7 6 5 4 3 2 1

Contents

PART ONE

An Introduction to Enterprise Systems

PART TWO

A New Environment for Enterprise Systems

PART THREE

Building Enterprise Systems

PART FOUR

Extending Enterprise Systems

Foreword

This book, written by professors at a university that has long been a leader in information systems education, is about the most important trend in information systems and organizations of the last decade: integration. At the beginning of the 1990s, companies were just beginning to reengineer their business processes. Their information systems were standalone, stovepiped applications that couldn't communicate with each other within the organization, much less externally with the systems of customers or suppliers.

But the 1990s was the decade of integration, and by the end of the decade and the early part of the new century, the world had changed. Many large firms had tried to implement cross-functional systems of their own making, but had later realized that broad enterprise applications packages were the way to implement reengineered processes. Having made substantial progress toward putting these packages in place, organizations began to work on extending and realizing the benefits from these systems. The rise of the Internet meant that firms had to connect the enterprise systems in their back offices with electronic commerce applications at the front end. And the vast amount of high-quality transaction data produced by enterprise systems meant that firms had to begin analyzing the information and using it to manage their businesses more effectively.

The entire journey toward business and systems integration is addressed within this book. The authors start simply, with discussions of why organizations need to be integrated in the first place and how these organizations became disintegrated. They also address the technological developments that led to islands of disconnected information. After the student or reader has understood how we got to the need for enterprise integration, the authors describe the present environment.

One of the most difficult aspects of creating and managing enterprise systems is combining all of the diverse pieces and competencies that an organization requires to be successful. The authors address in detail the technology architecture, data environment, and business process capabilities necessary to implement and profit from an enterprise system. The reader of

Enterprise Integration will learn how to assemble these diverse components to make an integrated whole.

While it's exciting to redesign a business with these new tools, it's all too tempting to stay at the 30,000-foot level of strategy, enterprise technology architecture, and high-level process designs. But the authors know that the real work of enterprise systems involves getting your hands dirty. They delve into such day-to-day necessities as balancing the load across different components of a system, normalizing databases, and backing up data. The reader gets both the big and the detailed, down-to-earth picture.

Many books about technology in business focus only on the technologies themselves within an information system and neglect the human factors in technology-enabled change. But *Enterprise Integration* doesn't forget that it's people who make these systems work. There is an admirable focus on change management, on roles and responsibilities throughout a project, and the importance of such external entities as consultants and vendors.

And the book is not abstract. There are plenty of examples of companies with real problems and real successes. Helpful checklists are provided for actually following through with an enterprise systems project, and clear diagrams abound. Actual vendors and their products are discussed.

In this era of techno-hype, its far too easy to get carried away about the Internet and electronic commerce. While the authors give these technologies their due, they don't go overboard. They wisely point out that even where e-business is concerned, it's the "backend integration" issues that companies find most difficult to deal with.

In short, the authors have produced a clear, cogent, and comprehensive guide to the all-important topic of integrated enterprise systems. Everything you'd want—from initial concept to effective implementation and use—is here. In other words, keep reading!

Thomas H. Davenport
Director, Accenture Institute for Strategic Change
Distinguished Scholar in Residence, Babson College
Visiting Professor, Tuck School of Business, Dartmouth College

Preface

Recent years have brought sweeping changes in the way organizations apply information technology to solve complex problems that are common in increasingly competitive and global business environments. In the past, deployment of information technology in most large firms led to manifold information systems operating independently and often redundantly throughout these enterprises. The inefficiencies and opportunity costs inherent in such "islands of automation" have forced many organizations to rethink their information technology strategies in the direction of enterprisewide integrated information systems.

Responding to the shift in how organizations use information technology—and indeed, how they use information—some business schools have been reinventing their core curricula. Forward-thinking schools are placing less emphasis on building narrow functional expertise in their students and more on developing an integrative understanding of business and business organizations. Many of these schools are answering a call from industry to provide students with practical experience using enterprise systems by joining alliances with enterprise software companies.

So, the need for instruction is clear. The resources have been flowing from software and hardware vendors. And the students are certainly ready and seemingly insatiable. But where are the textbooks and instructional materials? The reality is that, until now, most instructors have relied on conceptually lean trade publications, perhaps supplemented with packets of materials culled from the business and technology press. At long last, here is a textbook that begins to fill the gap.

Goals for This Book

This book aims to introduce students to enterprise systems. An enterprise system is an extraordinarily complex application of information technology designed to support organizational processes in a highly integrated fashion. The authors believe that learning about enterprise systems must begin with a strong conceptual grounding in the underlying technologies, organizations, and their processes, and most importantly, integration itself.

Enterprise Integration is intended to be an introductory book on the topic. Its target audience is undergraduate students majoring in information systems or business majors in a technically strong business school. The book could also serve well in an IS-oriented masters or MBA course. In addition, the book could support corporate training programs. Regardless of academic level or institutional setting, the book will work best where an enterprise system is installed and/or available to students.

The text begins by introducing the reader to enterprise systems, describing the organizational and technical context for their development, and exploring the challenges associated with their deployment and use. Next, business processes are explained, and an overview of basic components and typical architecture of an enterprise system is provided. Then, the text describes the processes through which organizations plan, design, realize, and operate enterprise systems. Finally, extensions to enterprise systems are discussed, including extended supply chain management, customer relationship management, e-commerce integration, managerial support systems, inter-enterprise integration, and global systems.

Features of the Book

Enterprise Integration has many innovative features designed to stimulate an interesting learning environment:

- Process orientation – Emphasis on understanding business processes. Understanding enterprise integration requires a coming to grips with the complexity of business processes operating within a firm as well as those spanning its relationships with external business partners. Students need to understand conceptually how linkages form between business processes and how these linkages are supported in an enterprise system.
- Brand-neutrality - Rather than teaching how to implement a specific brand of ERP software, the text focuses on enterprise systems in general. The result is a flexible, brand-neutral approach to the general application of enterprise systems.
- Experienced authors – The book's authors bring many decades of information systems and operations management experience to the text,

including countless hours working on enterprise systems implementations and ERP software.

Supplements

A number of valuable supplements are available to those who adopt *Enterprise Integration,* including:

- Much more than an ordinary textbook web site, adopters and their students will be entitled to membership in a highly interactive online community with articles, exercises, and resources related to enterprise systems as well as events and activities to support material in the book. The site address is: www.wiley.com/college/sandoe.

- A complete set of PowerPoint slides to accompany each chapter of the text.

- A comprehensive test bank with over 200 multiple choice and true/false questions.

- Available soon will be ERP product/version specific exercise manuals. Check the web site for more details.

Acknowledgements

Horace Greeley would have been proud, for this book project was born in New York City and soon headed west. It all began at Fordham University, and we have Aditya Saharia to thank for the idea of creating such a textbook as well as his early contributions to it. Also at Fordham, Jaak Jurison, Christine Bullen, and Dean Sharon Smith were tremendously supportive of the project and the SAP initiative there.

As the project moved west to Chico State, the inspired leadership of Department Chair Valerie Milliron helped to create the perfect climate for the book to develop. Jim Connolly contributed his knowledge and talent to the database chapter. We thank Jim Mensching for his determination in building the SAP program. We are indebted to Daniel Karl Gribschaw for his brilliant work as researcher early in the project, and Tom Wilder for helping to realize these ideas in course content and lab exercises with the assistance of George Lefkowitz, Marcus Gribschaw, and Adam Valentiner. We are truly grateful to our students for teaching us and for making teaching an enjoyable and honorable profession.

We would like to thank SAP America, its University Alliance, and both Dan Pantaleo, Vice President, Institute for Innovation and Development and Amelia Maurizio, Director, Higher Learning Initiatives at SAP America for their incredible commitment to supporting academic programs throughout this country and region.

We are grateful to the team of reviewers who offered their insight and suggestions during the writing of this book, and ultimately had a major impact on the shape of the finished book:

- Satya P. Chattopadhyay, University of Scranton
- Paul H. Cheney, University of Central Florida
- Laurentiu David, Centennial College
- James K. Hightower, California State University, Fullerton
- Richard A. Johnson, Southwest Missouri State University
- Catherine K. Murphy, Central Missouri State University
- Alfred Quinton, The College of New Jersey
- Judy Scott, University of Texas at Austin
- Simon Sharpe, University of Calgary
- E. Burton Swanson, UCLA
- Stephen L. Tracy, University of South Dakota
- Iris Vessey, Indiana University
- Edward F. Watson, Louisiana State University

We extend our thanks to those at Wiley who ultimately made this book possible (and publishable!). Acquisitions Editor Beth Lang Golub deserves our warmest gratitude for her extraordinary patience and flexibility. We also thank her sequence of able assistants Samantha Alducin and Jennifer Battista. Marketing dynamo, Jessica Garcia provided tremendous forward momentum for the book, and Senior Production Editor Christine Cervoni's attention to detail was essential in keeping the entire project on track. We would like to thank Maddy Lesure for her design advice and the superb cover design, and Gert Jan Hofstede for his wonderful illustration, not to mention his unrestrained Finnish tango.

Finally, our deepest gratitude goes to our families—parents, children, and spouses—whose encouragement and love made this work possible. We especially wish to thank Ray's wife Shelley for her unconditional support, Gail's children Kenny and Robyn for being there no matter what, and Kent's wife Heather for her patience and understanding through it all.

About the Authors

Kent Sandoe is an Associate Professor of Management Information Systems at California State University, Chico, where he teaches corporate information technology and electronic commerce. Kent has over 20 years of experience in the information systems area as a programmer, analyst, manager, and consultant. He has worked in a variety of industries, primarily within the transportation and financial services sectors. Recently, he worked within the Internet Commerce IT group at Cisco Systems where he conducted research on payments technologies. Prior to joining Chico State, Kent was on the faculty of the Graduate School of Business at Fordham University in New York City where he worked on SAP and e-commerce initiatives. Kent's research interests include organizational memory, information systems security, and institutional impacts of IT. He received his Ph.D. in Management Information Systems from Claremont Graduate University.

Gail Corbitt is a Professor of Management Information Systems at California State University, Chico, where she teaches software development and enterprise systems. Gail has over 20 years of experience in the information systems area. She has worked on major SAP implementation projects at Chevron and Hewlett Packard. In addition, she has been an active researcher and consultant in the areas of business process redesign, rapid/joint applications development, and collaborative group technology for numerous organizations including the U.S. Navy, Intel, BASF, Simpson Paper Company, California Prison Authority, and the Huber Company. She received her Ph.D. in Management Information Systems from the University of Colorado at Boulder.

Raymond Boykin is a Professor of Operations Management at California State University, Chico, where he is the Director of the SAP Program and coordinator of the Production and Operations Management option. Ray has published many articles in the areas of operations management, risk assessment and management, and quality management. His current research interests are enterprise systems, supply chain management, and business process analysis and reengineering. Prior to joining the faculty at Chico State, Ray held positions at PLG, Monsanto, and Rockwell International. His industry experience includes: SAP R/3 (MM and QM modules) implementation and configuration, quality data warehouse, production planning models for manufacturing operations, warehouse management, material quality control, and outbound logistics. Ray received his Ph.D. in Business Administration (Management Science) at St. Louis University.

About Chico State and the SAP University Alliance

In June of 1996, SAP America, Inc., the world leader in enterprise business software systems, selected the College of Business at California State University, Chico, as its first partner in the SAP University Alliance Program. By the end of 2000, SAP had entered into partnerships with more than 100 universities in the Americas. SAP established its University Alliance Program to accomplish the following:

- Expose students and faculty to SAP technology
- Increase the supply of technically qualified persons in the marketplace
- Hire high quality graduates who are knowledgeable in SAP technology
- Establish long-term research partnerships with universities
- Leverage student projects, faculty research, and student and faculty internships

Under the terms of the program, SAP provides universities with the most current version of the R/3 software, technical support, and training. Universities, in turn, commit to introducing the R/3 software in their curricula and to providing the support necessary to administer the system and enhance curricula.

Since the initial contacts with SAP America at the beginning of 1995, California State University, Chico (CSU, Chico) has dedicated itself to being a leader in the SAP University Alliance. The SAP program at CSU, Chico is the largest academic SAP program in the Americas. The program has integrated the R/3 software into more than 20 courses at the undergraduate and graduate level. Currently, over 1500 students per semester log on to one of the more than 20 instances of the SAP R/3 system. The hardware supporting the SAP program includes over 50 servers, from large HP UNIX servers (8 processors) to smaller Window NT servers. The current aggregate disk space is over 3 terabytes.

In 2000, CSU, Chico became the first SAP University Competency Center (UCC) in the United States currently serving four other universities.

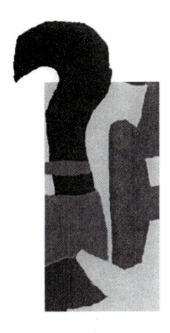

An Introduction to Enterprise Systems

The goal of the first part of the book is to orient the reader to the study of enterprise systems. The chapters in this part begin with some basic definitions and conceptual frameworks, provide an historical context on the use of information systems in organizations, and discuss the challenges facing organizations as they move toward integrating these systems.

Chapter 1

Information Systems, Organizations, and Integration

Some books are to be tasted, others are to be swallowed, and some few are to be chewed and digested. — Francis Bacon

This book is first and foremost about information systems. However, because information systems do not operate in isolation, it is also a book about organizations in which information systems function. Finally, it is a book about integration and the development of integrated information systems in organizational settings.

Since this work is about information systems, organizations, and integration, it is critical that the reader share our particular understanding of these terms. Thus, we begin this chapter with definitions of these terms, leading to the elaboration of a model of integrated information systems in organizations that will provide an organizing framework for the book. We then review the major topics covered in each chapter of the book. The chapter concludes with a discussion of the importance of the study of integrated information systems.

OBJECTIVES

- Define key terms

- Present model of integrated information systems

- Provide overview of book

- Discuss why the study of enterprise systems is important

What Is an Information System?

The term "information system" is used in many different ways within many different settings. Information systems are commonly associated with computers, but it is taken for granted that information systems are more than just computers. Often, a distinction is made between information technology and information systems—in a simple view, information technology comprises the "hard" stuff (computer hardware, networks, etc.) and information systems make up the "soft" things (software, data, applications, etc.). A more sophisticated way of drawing the distinction is to say that information technology consists of generic resources—computer hardware, software, networks, databases—widely available in the environment, whereas information systems represent specific applications tied to specific organizational situations.

This distinction reflects a new view of information technology as a collection of resources that are used to support people engaged in meaningful organizational activities. In fact, the term "IT resources" is becoming a common way to refer to information technology, while the term

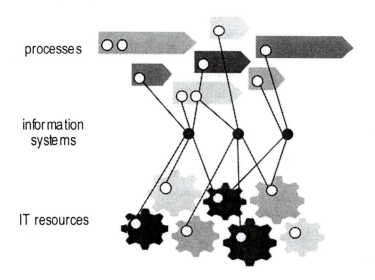

FIGURE 1-1. Information systems.

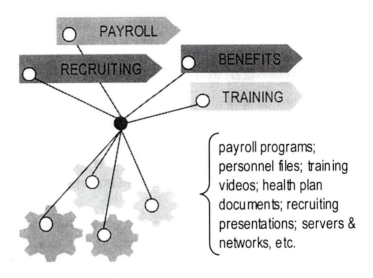

payroll programs;
personnel files; training
videos; health plan
documents; recruiting
presentations; servers &
networks, etc.

FIGURE 1-2. Example of a human resources information system.

"organizational process" or "business process" refers to a grouping of activities that people engage in within organizations.

So now we come to our definition of an information system:

> **An INFORMATION SYSTEM is a unique configuration of IT resources and organizational processes whereby the IT resources (and the information they provide) are applied to support specific organizational processes.**

This definition of information system emphasizes the linkage between process and technology in organizations. Clearly, information systems are more than technology; they involve some element of human activity. The definition can be represented graphically as shown in Figure 1-1. This diagram shows three layers: (1) organizational processes which represent the purposeful activity that is supported by the (2) information systems that generate the necessary information for the processes that they support using the (3) IT resources to store, transform, and transmit this information.

An example of our definition of information system is shown in Figure 1-2. Here, human resource processes are supported through the application of IT resources in a configuration called a human resources information system.

What Is an Organization?

As noted earlier, information systems do not exist in vacuums—their context is organizations. So, we define "organization" quite simply:

> **An ORGANIZATION is a group of people engaged in some form of purposeful activity that extends over time.**

Now let's take a closer look at each part of this definition. Obviously, an organization must consist of a group—an organization cannot be a single person. We say that the activity of an organization is "purposeful," meaning that an organization is defined in part by the ends it pursues: making a profit, serving a community, fulfilling a charter, and so on. Finally, we claim that an organization's activities must extend over time—there must be some continuity to an organization: otherwise it is just a mob.

An organization is made up of three components: people, processes, and structures. While the first component, people, is pretty well understood, organizational processes are rather complex. Thomas H. Davenport, a widely respected authority on enterprise systems, defines a process as: "A specific ordering of work activities across time and place, with a beginning, an end, and clearly identified inputs and outputs" (Davenport, 1993, p. 5).

Structures form the bases of coordination and control within organizations. They specify how communication occurs and where power and authority are distributed. Structures may be formally articulated in an organization's procedures manuals, organization charts, and other places, but they also exist informally, as is the case with unofficial social networks within an organization.

Organizations are not islands. They operate in environments made up of individuals, institutions, and other organizations. Many of the entities in an organization's environment have a stake in the organization's future and are known as stakeholders. Stakeholders can have a direct or indirect influence on an organization and can be directly or indirectly influenced

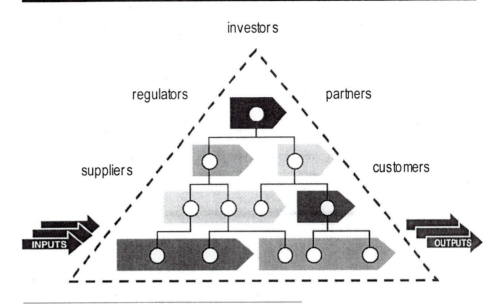

FIGURE 1-3. Organization and environment.

by it. Examples of stakeholders include suppliers, customers, partners, regulators, and investors.

Figure 1-3 is a schematic representation of an organization within its environment. It includes the three major components of organizations: people (circles), processes (arrows), and structures (lines).

What Is Integration?

Webster's dictionary defines integration as "To make whole or complete by adding or bringing together parts." Although many forms of integration exist, we are specifically interested in the integration of information systems. In the next chapter, you will learn about how information systems are often isolated from one another within organizations, causing numerous problems. Information systems integration involves bringing together previously isolated information systems with the goal of providing a more whole or complete information resource for the organization. The result is referred to as an enterprisewide information system, or enterprise system for short.

Integrated information systems are often achieved using Enterprise Resource Planning (ERP) software. This complex software forms the basis for integrating organizational information systems but is usually insufficient by itself. Integration is best achieved through a combination of technical and organizational process innovations. On a technical level, integration relies on the use of industry-standard common databases and common communication protocols. On the organizational process level, integration requires the simplification and streamlining of organizational processes using techniques such as business process reengineering and workflow redesign.

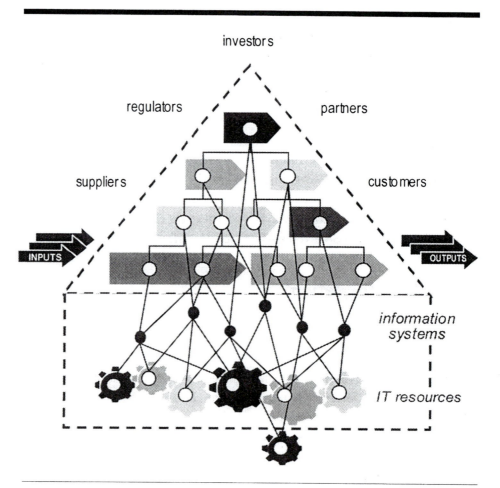

FIGURE 1-4. Information systems in organizational context.

A Model of Information Systems in Organizations

Now that we have defined the key terms—information system, organization, and integration—we will combine them into a model of information systems in organizations that will become a roadmap for the rest of the book. Figure 1-4 represents information systems in organizations. As you can see, the figure combines the representation of information system (Figure 1-1) with the representation of organization and environment (Figure 1-3).

In Figure 1-4, information systems link IT resources and organizational processes, as is also shown in Figure 1-1. This time, however, the processes and, as a result, the information systems are represented hierarchically to indicate different levels of managerial control and different types of information systems used to support these control levels.

Part of the IT resources resides outside the organizational boundary in the bottom of Figure 1-4. This is to reflect the fact that organizations are increasingly relying on IT resources that are not directly in their control such as public data resources, outsourced services, and the Internet.

Plan for the Book

The book comprises four parts: *An Introduction to Enterprise Systems, A New Environment for Enterprise Systems, Building Enterprise Systems,* and *Extending Enterprise Systems.*

In the present part, *An Introduction to Enterprise Systems,* the reader is provided with an historical context on the use of information systems in organizations as well as a discussion of the challenges facing organizations as they move toward integrating these systems. Following this introductory chapter, the second chapter in this section describes how modern organizations developed through the later part of the twentieth century, the rapid advancement of information technologies, and the fragmented nature of information systems in most organizational settings. The third chapter discusses the challenge of integration in terms of the motivations for integration, the common obstacles to achieving integrated systems, and some of the actual benefits of integrated systems.

The second part, *A New Environment for Enterprise Systems,* introduces the reader to enterprisewide integrated systems through an examination of each of the components that comprise them. The first chapter in this section defines organizational processes and describes how they interact to create chains of activity both inside and outside of organizations. The next chapter discusses how information technologies are arrayed as increasingly distributed resources within organizations. The reader is introduced to contemporary paradigms in distributed component architectures and client-server technologies. The third chapter in this section provides an introduction to database technologies that form the foundation for enterprise systems. The section concludes with a chapter that outlines the typical architecture of an enterprise system.

The third part, *Building Enterprise Systems*, shows the reader the processes through which organizations plan for, design, deploy, and operate enterprise systems. The first chapter in this section provides an overview of the enterprise system implementation life cycle and then focuses on the project initiation phase, including sourcing and vendor selection strategies, deployment options, and the establishment of the project charter. The following chapter covers the next two phases of enterprise system implementation: planning and design. Here, the reader is introduced to implementation project management as well as the various tools and methodologies available during the planning and design phases. The chapter also discusses enterprise modeling, including techniques for defining enterprise structure and the implications for reinventing or reengineering the organization. The next chapter in this section provides a step-by-step description of the realization of enterprise systems, beginning with customizing for different organizational structures and defining company-specific objects, continuing with populating databases, building interfaces with the legacy systems, and defining customized reports, and concluding with testing and end-user acceptance. The chapter also covers the often neglected, but critical, topic of enterprise systems maintenance, including discussion of administration, metrics and tuning, training, and quality assurance. The section concludes with a chapter on people in enterprise systems. This chapter describes changing roles in the information systems area as well as other areas within the enterprise, discusses the various career paths that appear most promising, and describes the influence of gurus and mentors, executive sponsorship, and team-based structures in enterprise systems.

In the final part, *Extending Enterprise Systems*, the reader gets a glimpse of the many directions in which enterprise systems are being extended within organizations. The first chapter in this theme covers backward integration, including a discussion of extended supply chain management, procurement systems, and other interorganizational systems. The next chapter focuses on forward integration and the demand chain, with a discussion of Internet-enabled enterprise systems, customer asset management, sales force automation, and channel management systems. The final chapter discusses extending enterprise systems to support managers and executives through decision analysis tools, executive information systems, and data warehouses.

Why Is This Important?

One might question the value of placing such an emphasis on a single class of information systems—enterprise systems. What is so special about them? Why do they merit such close examination?

It is our claim that the study of enterprise systems is both intrinsically and extrinsically valuable. Intrinsically, enterprise systems are worth studying because they are at the core of organizational computing. Unlike peripheral systems such as office automation software in most companies, enterprise systems inform the critical processes that organizations depend on for their success. Furthermore, enterprise systems by their very design have the broadest reach of all organizational information systems—they are used by every major functional area and at all levels of the enterprise.

Extrinsically, enterprise systems are worth studying because they represent a fundamental shift in the way that most organizations use information systems. Enterprise systems are a broad phenomenon; no longer are they being deployed solely in extremely large companies, nor are they being used just in certain industries.

Because of their high degree of complexity and the fact that organizations are increasingly dependent on the smooth operation of these systems for their success, the sophisticated skills needed to implement and manage enterprise systems are among the most sought after among computing professionals today.

References

Davenport, Thomas H. *Process Innovation: Reengineering Work through Information Technology.* Cambridge, Mass.: Harvard Business School Press, 1993, p. 5.

Webster's New 20th Century Unabridged, Second Edition. New York: Simon & Schuster, 1983.

Chapter 2

Silos, Mousetraps, and Islands: A Chronicle of Information Systems in Organizations

History is a relentless master. It has no present, only the past rushing into the future. To try to hold fast is to be swept aside. — John Fitzgerald Kennedy

OBJECTIVES

- Provide an historical context for understanding enterprise systems

- Explain failures in organizations, information technology, and the management of information systems

- Discover conditions that foster efforts to build integrated information systems

We live in a time of tremendous progress. Not only have we built marvelous tools for collecting, managing, and using information, but also we have developed extraordinary ways to organize ourselves and our activities around these tools to achieve unparalleled economic progress. As we scan the horizon, the possibilities for the future appear boundless. But our ability to see accurately into the future is limited by our understanding of the past.

The goal of this chapter is to provide readers with a sense of the context for organizations, information technology, and information systems. We describe this context in terms of both advances and failures that set the stage for enterprise integration.

We begin by discussing how organizations grow, divide their labor, and develop systems of coordination and control ultimately leading to silo-bound organizations. Next, we describe advances in computer-based information technology that has led to a glut of better mousetraps, and we show how these proprietary technologies don't connect. Finally, we discuss the development of information systems and how their uneven management has produced islands of automation throughout the enterprise.

Organizations as Functional Silos

If you look around, you will see that your world is full of organizations. Like most people, you probably are a member of several organizations: your work, your school, your bank, your club, your municipality. The fact is that most human activity takes place in organizations. If we look closer, it is easy to see that there are many types of organizations. Some are big while others are small; some are organized for profit while others are nonprofit; some are very traditional while others are modern. Organizations operate in different industries, and organizations serve different purposes. But why do they exist? And why do they look the way they do?

The Development of Modern Organizations

The development of modern organizations has been characterized as an outgrowth of the struggle to reconcile two opposing forces. On the one hand, there is the desire to accrue the tremendous advantages that are achieved through the specialization of work. This is known as the division of labor. The advantages of division of labor include:

- The ability to manage complexity—dividing a problem into its component parts, solving each in turn, and then resolving them into a total solution is a standard problem-solving technique (aka "divide and conquer").

- The ability to achieve mastery—specializing in a particular task area—generally leads to better performance (greater speed, fewer mistakes, higher quality) and eventually to mastery of the task (aka "do one thing, and do it well").

THE LEGEND OF WALLY

Once upon a time, there was a guy named Wally. As a teenager, Wally really enjoyed riding his bicycle. Even more than riding, he loved to tinker with his bicycle. After working one summer at a local bike shop, he decided to drop out of junior college and start building bicycles in his garage. In no time, he got to be very good at it, and he had no trouble selling them at the weekend swap meet.

Pretty soon, lots of people wanted to buy his bicycles, and he was having trouble keeping up with their orders. So Wally managed to convince his former high school buddy, Spike, to join him, and for a while the two of them were able to keep up with a steadily increasing stream of orders. As things got busier, they split up the work, with Wally cutting, jigging, and welding the frames while Spike sanded, painted, and assembled the finished bikes. The two worked around a large workbench in the middle of the garage so they could easily talk to and assist each other whenever necessary.

It soon became clear that they needed more help, so Wally hired three people whom he knew from the local bicycle club, trained them each in a different aspect of the bike-making process, and put them to work. At first, he monitored their work closely, but when he realized that they appeared competent and that he didn't really have time, he appointed Spike to make sure that every finished bike met their expectations for quality.

Sales continued to grow and Wally needed more help, but this time he decided to hire three recent graduates from the metal-working program of a local trade school. This way, he wouldn't have to spend as much time training them as he had with Spike and the others, and he could devote more of his time to running the business. Space in the garage was getting a bit cramped, so they soon moved into an industrial park and hired three more employees.

As CEO of Wally's Wheels, Inc., Wally found he was spending most of his time meeting with dealers and distributors, so he promoted Spike to factory manager and singled out the brightest of the recent trade school hires to be trained on the new computer-aided design software that Wally had purchased at a recent trade show. Wally was never good at numbers, so he was relieved when Spike's sister Bernice came on board as a full-time bookkeeper.

Within three years, business was so successful that Wally decided to diversify with a new division that made skateboards in the summer and snowboards in the winter. Shortly thereafter, Wally opened manufacturing plants in Mexico and Indonesia, set up distribution centers in Europe and Australia, sponsored several major bicycling and snowboarding events, and renamed his company "Wally's World of Wheels" to reflect its global character.

It wasn't long before Wally was sitting behind a polished mahogany desk in his office on the twelfth floor of the WWW Enterprises building thinking about the changes he'd experienced in recent years. Part of him was sad that he hadn't been on a bicycle in three years, but another part of him was excited about this new thing that he'd read about on an airplane that was going to revolutionize his business. And he wondered why they called it the web....

- Reduced task-switching time—stopping one task, shifting focus and equipment to a different task, and commencing work on the new task can involve a great deal of overhead in terms of time, mental and physical energy, and adjustment of resources that can be decreased with specialization.

- Reduced training costs—if all workers do every task, training new employees can be very costly, as opposed to training employees on a single task.

- Scalability of the workforce—the ability to increase (or decrease) the workforce in units related to specific task areas gives an organization a great deal of flexibility in meeting demand and responding to environmental changes.

On the other hand, these advantages must be balanced by the need to coordinate and control these work activities. The greater the degree of work specialization, the more subdivided the labor, the more difficult it is to control and coordinate these activities.

Organizational Design and Theories of Control

Organizational theorists have advanced many hypotheses on how specialized organizational activity is coordinated. According to the American school of scientific management which theorized at the turn of the twentieth century (Taylor, 1911), coordination and control were best achieved in modern industrial organizations through the standardization of work processes. The views of scientific management are epitomized by the automobile assembly line where the careful sequencing of standardized tasks resulted in productivity gains that revolutionized industrial society on a global scale. In a different vein, German sociologist Max Weber theorized that rules, job descriptions, and formal training were the bases for coordination and control. He believed that the modern bureaucratic model that he described was the most rational, efficient, and legitimate form of organization and one to which all should aspire (Weber, 1958).

While both Weber's and the scientific school's views on organizational coordination and control are essentially sound, management theorist Henry Mintzberg provides a more complete description. He argues that most organizations use a set of coordinating mechanisms in varying combinations

3 PEOPLE = 3 CHANNELS

6 PEOPLE = 15 CHANNELS

12 PEOPLE = 66 CHANNELS

FIGURE 2-1. Communications channels increase exponentially as people increase.

depending on the organization's age, size, purpose, and environment (Mintzberg, 1979). The basic mechanisms that Mintzberg describes are:

- Mutual adjustment—where tasks are coordinated through informal communication, simply by the workers talking with one another.
- Direct supervision—whereby one worker (the supervisor) becomes responsible for the work of others and directs them by issuing instructions and monitoring their activities.
- Standardization of tasks—where the content of the tasks is specified in detail ahead of time, either through written or oral instructions or in conjunction with some form of production technology such as the conveyor belt in an assembly line.
- Standardization of outputs—whereby the results of the work are specified, such as a product's dimensions, performance characteristics, or quality.
- Standardization of skills—where the knowledge, abilities, or training necessary to complete the tasks is specified.

Stages of Organizational Growth

Most organizations, like Wally's, start small and grow. Not all organizations grow at the same rate, and individual organizations often grow at different rates at different times. But grow they do, and with successful organizations, growth can be the most significant force in determining their character (Blau, 1955).

In a very small organization—such as Wally's when just he and Spike ran the show—there is no need for elaborate coordination mechanisms. Mutual adjustment through informal communication—Wally and Spike chattering to each other across the workbench—is usually sufficient. But at some point, at some magic number of people, informal communication doesn't work any more. This is because every additional employee almost doubles the number of conversations or channels that the informal network must support (see Figure 2-1).

Eventually, mutual adjustment must be superseded by an alternative mechanism of coordination, usually some form of direct supervision—Wally monitoring the work of his new employees. This may give way or be augmented by standardization of tasks, standardization of outputs—Spike

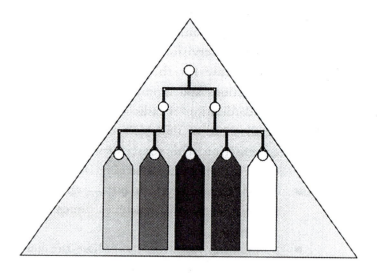

FIGURE 2-2. Functional organization.

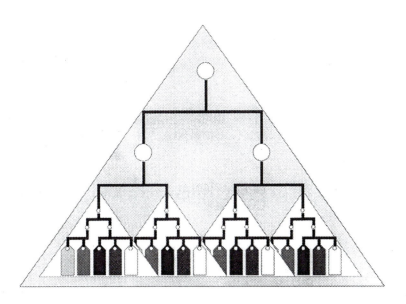

FIGURE 2-3. Divisionalized organization.

as quality control—or standardization of skills—Wally hiring trade school grads.

As an organization grows, employees are typically grouped into departments based on the type of work they do. This task-based grouping is the basis for modern functionally structured organizations. In a functionally structured organization, employees are typically assigned to departments such as finance, manufacturing, distribution, sales, human resources, and information systems. This is the most common form of organization for small companies as well as for the base units within large organizations (see Figure 2-2).

In many organizations, functional areas as well as individual positions are characterized as either line or staff. A line function or position is one that is directly related to the primary goals of the firm. A staff function or position serves a secondary or support role in the organization. Examples of line functions are production, finance, and marketing. Staff functions include such areas as human resources and research and development, while

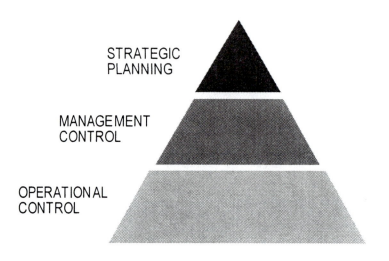

FIGURE 2-4. Anthony's model.

examples of staff positions include administrative assistants and legal advisors.

For large organizations that operate in many regions of the globe and offer many widely divergent products and/or services, the functional form is superseded by a higher order grouping based on many possible factors, the most common of which are product and location. The divisionalized form that results from diversification, globalization, or other factors is highly complex, with power that is commonly dispersed to the operating divisions giving them a great deal of autonomy. The divisions themselves are typically organized functionally, resulting in a structure like that shown in Figure 2-3.

The Composition of Organizations

Anthony (1965) described the parts of organizations by grouping them according to the type of decision making that was required. He defined three levels: strategic, managerial control, and operational control. Although simplistic, Anthony's model has been the dominant vehicle for understanding and classifying information systems and decision-support tools in organizations for several decades (see Figure 2-4).

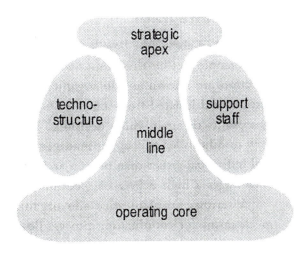

FIGURE 2-5. Mintzberg's form.

Mintzberg (1983) expanded on Anthony's three-level model by adding two components that would typically be grouped under staff functions, the technostructure and support staff. His parts of the organization and the people included in each are outlined here and shown in Figure 2-5.

- Operating core – this consists of the workers who actually carry out the productive work of the organization.
- Strategic apex – this is made up of the top management team and focuses on achieving the organization's mission.
- Middle line – this part comprises middle- and lower-level managers who form the chain of authority between the operating core and strategic apex.
- Technostructure – this consists of analysts such as engineers, accountants, and planners focused on standardization of tasks, outputs, and skills.
- Support staff – these are workers who provide any of a variety of types of support not directly related to production. These workers may be

employed to support any level of the enterprise (e.g., legal counsel, bookkeeping, food services).

A Failure to Integrate

As described above, the base level of most organizations groups the activities of its employees by their function. Organizations that group activities by function are known as silo organizations because each functional area is distinct and isolated from all other functional areas with limited entry and exit points through which decisions, information, and goods and services flow to other silos and upper management. Silo organizations focus on task and individual rather than process and team, and their grouping by function encourages a high degree of specialization.

A serious problem with silo organizations is their limited built-in mechanisms for coordinating process flows that cross boundaries from one functional area to another. As long as things are running perfectly smoothly, this is usually not a serious deficiency. But when there is a breakdown in the process flow caused by an exception or unusual occurrence that requires an integrated solution, the functional organization has difficulty coping. For example, if a supplier of a critical part fails to deliver an order to a manufacturing plant because of a breakdown between procurement and accounts payable, the problem must work its way up within each functional area (manufacturing, procurement, and accounting) to a level on which the heads of these areas meet (an executive committee made up of the VPs of each area), forcing these executives who may have little genuine expertise in the area to micromanage a problem that is far removed from its origin. The result is often poor decisions, wasted time, and serious negative consequences for organizational performance.

Another problem that comes from grouping organizational activities into functional areas is a general loss of perspective. Although all employees have a clear idea of their responsibilities within their narrow functional domain, they may have little sense of the "big picture," of where the organization is going as a whole and how their activities contribute to moving it in its intended direction. Without highly developed planning and control from above coupled with continual indoctrination of employees in the company mission, the parochialism that the silo organization promotes may make it extremely difficult to keep an organization on track as each area pulls in its own direction.

Related to the loss of perspective in silo organizations is the difficulty in tracking overall performance or developing objectives that are directly tied to the goals of the firm. Certainly, each functional area can develop standards of performance that relate to the work activities within that area, but are these the ones that count? Which is a more important measure of success: sales, cash receipts on these sales, or long-term customer satisfaction? The first is a measure of productivity of the sales function and is easy to track in a silo organization. The second ties two functional areas together, sales and accounting, and is more complex but possible to track at a high level in a silo organization. The third measure—customer satisfaction—is very difficult to track in an objective sense when work is structured in a highly functional way. In upcoming chapters, we will learn how critical organizational performance measures—such as customer satisfaction—can be meaningfully and objectively measured at all levels of the integrated enterprise.

Technology that Computes, but Does not Connect

Most people associate information technology (IT) with computers. While this is clearly correct, IT can be viewed more broadly as any technology that informs us. And why limit ourselves to electronic technologies? Technology needn't be electronic; the plough, for example, was a technology that revolutionized the world in its time. So, information technologies must also admit books, pens, pencils, paper, and clay tablets. Some may go so far as to consider language itself to be IT in its earliest form.

But this doesn't help us too much. We need a narrower definition. Unfortunately, just placing "automated" or "electronic" in front of IT includes many technologies, radio and television among them, that are obviously beyond the scope of this discussion. Let's settle on computer-based IT as being equivalent for us with information technology per se.

Advances in Computer-Based IT

The past four decades have produced extraordinary and well-documented advances in computer-based IT. Most striking are the improvements in the

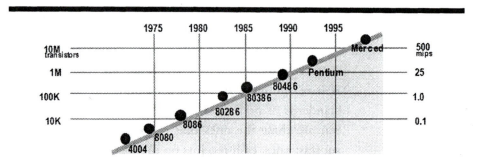

FIGURE 2-6. Microprocessor performance, 1988–2000.

price and performance of processors, memory, and storage media (see Figures 2-6 and 2-7).

Arguably as significant but less well-documented are the advances in the reliability and flexibility of many varieties of computer-based IT. It has become commonplace to talk of advances in computer technology in terms of "generations" (see Table 2-1).

The first generation of computer technology was characterized by the use of vacuum tubes and magnetic drums for data storage. The ENIAC (developed by John Eckert and John Mauchly) was the first general-purpose electronic computer based on this technology. It consisted of 18,000 vacuum tubes, 70,000 resistors, and 5 million soldered joints, and it consumed 160 kilowatts of electrical power (enough energy to dim the lights in an entire section of Philadelphia). Because its operating instructions had to

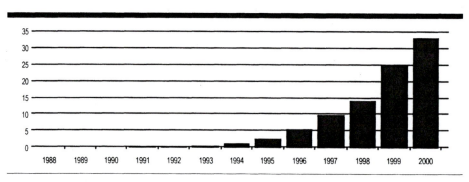

FIGURE 2-7. Disk capacity in megabytes per dollar, 1988–2000.

Generation	Timeframe	Key Innovation
1st Generation	1945–1956	Vacuum tube
2nd Generation	1956–1963	Transistor
3rd Generation	1964–1971	Integrated circuit
4th Generation	1971–Present	Large-scale integration

TABLE 2-1. Generations of computer-based information technology.

be custom-tailored using a complex binary code for each job, its versatility, speed, and overall usefulness were quite limited.

The second generation of computer technology came about thanks to the invention of the transistor in 1948. By replacing vacuum tubes with transistors, engineers were able to build computers that were smaller, faster, more reliable, and more energy-efficient than their vacuum tube ancestors. In addition to their solid state design, second-generation computers incorporated significant advances in magnetic-core memory as well as the concept of the programming language that made computers more flexible and thus more productive for business use. In fact, the successful commercial use of second-generation computers led a number of companies to start manufacturing and selling these large machines, including IBM, Sperry-Rand, Burroughs, and Honeywell.

The third generation of computer technology was made possible by the development of the integrated circuit. By placing a number of transistors and other components on a single chip, or semiconductor, engineers were able to reduce the amount of heat that was generated as well as the power consumed by even smaller computers. Another innovation that occurred was the creation of operating systems that allowed programs to be developed independently of the precise configuration of hardware that they were run

A TRAIN TO NOWHERE

Imagine that you are elected to the city council of a medium-sized city in northern Wisconsin. The constituents from your district have prevailed upon you to provide some sort of mass transit system to help reduce rush hour congestion. So you manage to find the funds to buy a used but powerful locomotive from a French company and have their engineers install several miles of tracks in and around your district. So, you're in business—until you discover that one of the districts adjoining yours recently bought a fleet of buses and another adjoining district just contracted with a Japanese firm to install a monorail. Now when your constituents want to travel across town, they will have to get off the train at the edge of your district, wait for a bus or monorail, and repeat this process using a new mode of transportation across each district until they reach their final destination.

To make matters worse, when winter hits, your constituents ask you to use the locomotive to provide shuttle service to Disney World in Florida. So you load everybody in the train and head south, only to discover that the next city over bought its transit system from a German company and the gauge of the tracks is different. Now you could swap out the wheels, but you find out that the next city bought a Dutch locomotive, and so on.

on. Operating systems also allowed a single computer to run multiple programs at once.

The fourth generation of computer technology did not involve one single key innovation as in prior generations. Instead, it involved the level of integration in semiconductor technology. Using large-scale integration (LSI), engineers could fit hundreds of components onto a single chip. The next step, very large-scale integration (VLSI), allowed hundreds of thousands of components on a chip. Finally, ultra-large-scale integration (ULSI) squeezed millions of components onto a chip. The result was to simultaneously reduce the size and price of computers while increasing their efficiency and reliability.

A Failure to Communicate

Despite the tremendous advances in all forms of information technology, the challenge of getting disparate computer technologies to talk to one another, to connect, has been and continues to be one of the most daunting problems facing both engineers and managers in organizations today. This

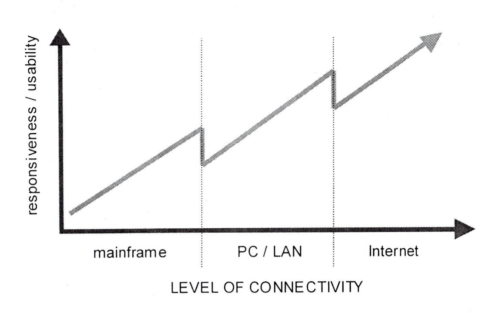

FIGURE 2-8. Connectivity and responsiveness in IT.

is because connectivity is not a purely technical issue. In fact, technology is the easy part. Much harder is overcoming organizational inertia, getting technical experts at all levels to agree on particular standards, and creating sufficient responsiveness in the systems themselves to compel users to want to connect.

In stable markets, organizational inertia is understandable even if it is often frustrating. There is no need for an organization to remake itself or reformulate its technological underpinnings when conditions aren't changing. In terms of IT, organizations that have invested huge sums in computer systems are likely to be reluctant to shed their technology like a fashion model changes clothes. Legacy systems exist in organizations as a reminder not only of the enormous price tag of these systems, but also of the even greater human resource cost in terms of training and expertise that is invested in them.

Technical standards are double-edged swords. On the one hand, technology, and in particular connective technology, cannot move forward

Era	Time Frame	Key Technology
Era I	1950 to late 1970s	Mainframe computers
Era II	late 1970s and 1980s	Proliferation of PCs
Era III	1990 to present	Networked enterprise

TABLE 2-2. Eras of information technology management.

without a solid foundation of standards. Yet, their very solidness results from the fact that standards represent a freezing of technology at a specific point in time. Progress depends on standards, while at the same time standards represent the end of progress. This dilemma means that standards take time to develop and be accepted; the more dynamic the technical area, the longer it takes for things to settle into a groove. In the absence of standards, proprietary technologies have a tendency to proliferate as everyone has a better idea for a better mousetrap. For information technologies, the resulting heterogeneity or diversity of platforms makes connectivity extremely difficult.

Finally, connectivity lags far behind other areas of IT performance because every time an attempt is made to connect diverse platforms, the usability or responsiveness of the information systems that depend on these platforms suffers. This is because the information systems that now must operate on the newly connected platform have their basic functionality reduced to the lowest common denominator. For example, the applications that ran on the earliest local area network (LAN) systems were abysmal in terms of features and responsiveness when compared to the equivalent applications that were available for stand-alone computer systems. Gradually, those LAN-based applications regained and even exceeded much of the usability that they lost when moving to an interconnected platform, only to have this functionality reduced again when the platform was expanded to include wide area network (WAN) systems or Internet connectivity. Indeed, the early browser-based platforms of the World Wide Web had very little of the functionality or richness of features that LAN-based applications had at the time, but gradually web technologies are gaining back lost ground and appear destined to meet or exceed the capabilities of today's LAN-based information systems (see Figure 2-8).

Information Systems as "Islands of Automation"

Until recently, information systems in organizations have been highly fragmented along functional lines. There are historical reasons for this that relate to both the configuration of organizations and the deployment of information technology within them. In this section, we explore the reasons information systems within organizations have become known as "islands of automation."

Advances in Information Systems

Just as there has been tremendous progress in information technology over the past 50 years, there have also been many advances in information systems. In particular, the acquisition and deployment of information systems in organizations have undergone radical change, as have the strategic management and use of data.

Applegate et al. (1999, pp. 25, 141) describe three eras of IT management that are defined in part by the computing devices and the people who had access to them (see Table 2-2).

The first era of IT management is characterized by centralized mainframes—enormous machines that were housed in specialized, air-conditioned data centers. These "glass houses" were staffed by data processing professionals and were led by data processing managers. Software development was commonly performed in-house by trained programmers using life cycle development methodologies. Data was managed in large hierarchical or network databases that were provided fast access but very little flexibility or compatibility. Data entry was done mostly through batch processes, and paper reports constituted the primary user interface. Applegate et al. describe the administrative framework of this era as a regulated monopoly with a focus on efficiency and productivity. IT was typically managed on a project-by-project basis, with close attention paid to return on investment (ROI) paybacks.

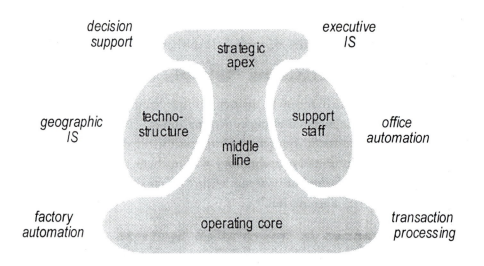

FIGURE 2-9. IS by part of organization supported.

The second era of IT management is characterized by the proliferation of PCs to the desktops of technical and nontechnical end users alike and massive decentralizing of the IS function within organizations. Software development was performed less and less by in-house development staff, and when it was, it was often based on nontraditional methodologies such as rapid prototyping and end-user development. Outsourcing became the rage for specialties previously controlled by the centralized data processing department ranging from development to operations and training. Data management focused on the widespread deployment of relational databases that often came in desktop versions that were accessible to ordinary users. Applegate et al. (1999) describe the administrative framework of this era as a free market. In this era, users no longer had to rely on a centralized data processing department for their information needs. Instead of efficiency as measured by ROI, the second era was more concerned with individual and group effectiveness.

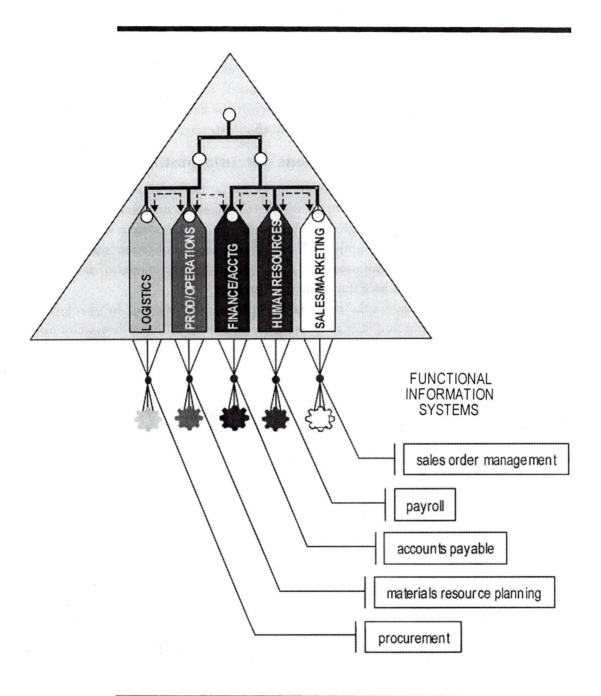

LOGISTICS

PROD/OPERATIONS

FINANCE/ACCTG

HUMAN RESOURCES

SALES/MARKETING

FUNCTIONAL
INFORMATION
SYSTEMS

sales order management

payroll

accounts payable

materials resource planning

procurement

FIGURE 2-10. IS by functional area supported.

The third era of IT management is largely the subject of later chapters of this book and is covered in much greater depth there. But peeking ahead, we see this era as characterized by networks comprised of powerful servers (sometimes mainframes) connected to a wide range of computational appliances reaching every corner of the enterprise. The managerial focus is on enterprise data and application integration and value creation.

Traditional Classifications for Information Systems

Since information systems are at least as diverse in size, scope, and function as the organizations in which they operate, academics and practitioners have long sought to classify them in ways that would further an understanding of them. The most common classification frameworks attempt to position information systems according to the level of the organization or the business functions they support.

Frameworks that classify information system by the level of the organization that these systems support usually divide systems according to the three levels of control proposed by Anthony (see Figure 2.4): operational control, managerial control, and strategic planning. We can expand on this by using Mintzberg's typology as shown in Figure 2.9.

Using Mintzberg's form, we can group systems according to whether they support operations (factory automation, transaction processing), managers (decision-support systems), executives (executive IS), or support staff and analysts (office automation). One limitation that becomes apparent in such a classification scheme is that many systems fall under multiple categories (e.g., office automation).

Another common approach to the classification of information systems is by the business function that the system supports (see Figure 2-10). Classifying IS according to functional area is a useful way to understand the fragmentation of IS within modern enterprises and demonstrates the value of trying to integrate these systems.

Later in the book we will see how both of these classification schemes—by level of control or by functional area—are clearly inadequate, and we will propose an alternative framework that helps us to understand the deployment and use of enterprisewide information systems.

A Failure to Allocate

With a fundamental shift in how computing is viewed in organizations from specialized tools to organizational resources, the central issue for IS management has become how to allocate them most appropriately within the organizational setting and beyond. Until recently, IS management in few organizations had come to grips with this issue, and the result was a tremendous imbalance in distribution of IT resources as the operating norm in organizations.

Although centralized IS management clung desperately to its traditional yet rapidly eroding power base of mainframe computing, there was a widespread emergence of information systems built to support specific functional areas of the enterprise. Sometimes these efforts were formally sanctioned, and at other times they began as unofficial or "rogue" computing efforts.

The result of this for most large organizations was the creation of "islands of automation"—information systems that serve functional areas of the enterprise without regard to sharing the information that these systems generate and provide to business processes housed within that functional area. The lack of "information bridges" in the IS archipelago becomes most pronounced when information is required to support processes that touch on more than one functional area. In these cases, data are transferred manually by means of paper reports leading to errors, redundant efforts, and limited ability to conduct any kind of detailed analysis.

Summary

The goal of this chapter was to give the reader a sense of the historical context for organizations, information technology, and information systems. We described the growth of modern organizations and the development of the silo organization. Next, we discussed the progress of computer-based information technology and the failure of these systems to provide connectivity. Finally, we described how information systems have become islands of automation throughout the enterprise. This will prepare the reader for the next chapter where we discuss the challenge of integration in terms of the motivations for integration, the common obstacles to achieving integrated systems, and some of the actual benefits of integrated systems.

Discussion Questions

1. Think about an organization of which you are a member or with which you interact frequently. How long has it existed? What purpose does it serve? Could the same purpose be served without an organization? Explain.

2. Why do organizations exist? Do some organizations exist today that no longer serve a real purpose? Why or why not?

3. What do the authors mean by "islands of automation?" What are the factors that lead an organization to create these islands? Give some examples.

4. Discuss the tradeoff between connectivity and responsiveness in information technology. Do you believe there are any limits to this relationship? What role does the Internet play in terms of connectivity and responsiveness?

5. Explain the role of standards in the development of information technology. What are some positive and negative aspects of the adoption of standards? How do these differ for IT developers and IT consumers?

References

Anthony, Robert N. *Planning and Control Systems: A Framework for Analysis.* Cambridge, Mass.: Harvard University, Graduate School of Business Administration, Division of Research, 1965.

Applegate, Lynda M., F. Warren McFarlan, and James L. McKenney. *Corporate Information Systems Management: The Challenges of Managing in an Information Age.* 5th edition. New York: McGraw-Hill, 1999.

Blau, Peter. *The Dynamics of Bureaucracy.* Chicago: University of Chicago Press, 1955.

Mintzberg, Henry. *The Structuring of Organizations.* Englewood Cliffs, N.J.: Prentice-Hall, 1979.

Mintzberg, Henry. *Structure in Fives: Designing Effective Organizations*. Englewood
    Cliffs, N.J.: Prentice-Hall, 1983.

Taylor, F.W. *Scientific Management*. New York: Harper and Row, 1911.

Weber, Max. *The Theory of Social and Economic Organization*. Trans. by A.M.
    Henderson and T. Parsons. New York: Oxford University Press, 1958.

Chapter 3

The Challenge of Integration

In the middle of difficulty lies opportunity. — Albert Einstein

Integrating the information systems across a large modern enterprise is by no means an easy task. It is a highly complex undertaking involving factors ranging from high tech to high touch. It is often very expensive, entailing unusually large exposure to financial risk because of its time-consuming and resource-intensive nature.

To better understand enterprise integration, this chapter begins with an exploration of some of the more common motivations for integration. Next, it is important to come to grips with many of the obstacles that companies embarking on such integration efforts are likely to face. Following a discussion of obstacles, we examine some of the tangible and intangible benefits of integration. Finally, we present some examples from industry that highlight some of the successes and failures of enterprise integration.

OBJECTIVES

♦ Explore organizational motivations for enterprise integration

♦ Understand common obstacles to integration

♦ Identify tangible and intangible benefits to integration

Motivation for Integration

To reiterate, the integration of information systems across the enterprise entails a large amount of risk. So, when a company is considering such a move, there must be serious and compelling reasons that counterbalance the risks. This section discusses some of the factors that motivate an organization toward enterprise integration.

There are two major categories of motivational factors for enterprise integration. First, an organization may choose to integrate because of its concerns about its operations, both with internal processes and external relationships (see Figure 3-1). Second, there are several compelling technical reasons for enterprise integration (see Figure 3-2).

Enterprise integration is viewed as a possible solution to a number of problems with internal organizational processes. Many organizations are concerned about controlling costs—in inventory, production, personnel, and almost every other area of the enterprise—and view integration efforts as one way to reduce their cost structures without sacrificing quality. To many organizations, their existing processes are overly complex and often ineffective and inconsistent. Enterprise integration is perceived as a way to

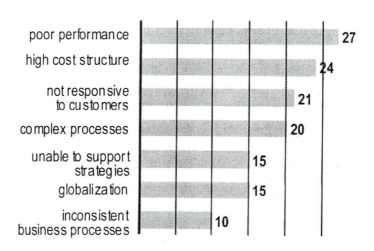

FIGURE 3-1. Operational motivations (adapted from DC 99).

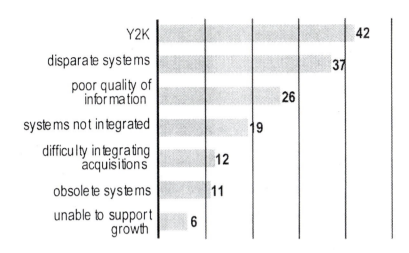

FIGURE 3-2. Technical motivations (adapted from DC 99).

streamline these processes and improve their overall effectiveness. Externally, enterprise systems seem to offer a vehicle for enhancing competitive performance, increasing responsiveness to customers, and supporting strategic initiatives. As business becomes increasingly global, integrated systems show promise for tying together the geographically dispersed organization.

Although the lack of Year 2000 compliance has been the major technological problem compelling organizations to move to enterprise systems, several other technical factors are considered motivators for integration. Foremost among these factors is the confusion of disparate systems, and integration is aimed at reducing this complexity. Another driving force is a concern about organizational information in terms of its quality and visibility. Lack of integration of existing systems or of those systems inherited through acquisition is sometimes the target of enterprise systems efforts. Finally, a move to enterprise systems is often a move away from prior systems that are approaching obsolescence or show little ability to support growth.

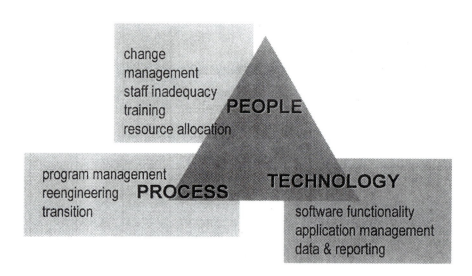

FIGURE 3-3. Obstacles to integration.

Obstacles to Achieving Integrated Systems

Despite the numerous motivational factors for enterprise systems, most organizations are aware that many potential stumbling blocks exist. The obstacles to integration can be grouped in three broad categories: people-related obstacles, process-related obstacles, and technology-related obstacles (see Figure 3-3).

Of the three kinds of obstacles to enterprise integration, by far the largest area of concern is that of people issues, and chief among people-related obstacles is change management. Integrating information systems across the organization is an enormous undertaking for all but the smallest of companies. In addition to being able to properly manage the change to integrated systems, people-related obstacles also extend to the capabilities of the internal staff as well as the project team, and these concerns are coupled with apprehension over the availability of adequate training resources. The prioritization and allocation of resources in general is a high concern that is often associated with support, or lack thereof, from top management.

A LUCKY QUARTER FOR YOUR DDS

Can you imagine, just days before Halloween, shopping for all those cute little fairy princesses and ghosts who will trick-or-treat at your door, and not having any Hershey's chocolates to pass out? No Reese's Peanut-Butter Cups, no Rolos, no bite-sized Kit Kats to share with your neighbors. Yes, in the Fall of 1999, Hershey Foods Corporation took a nose dive in the order-fulfillment department when they embarked on a $112 million ERP project just months before stores began to order their sweet treats for the biggest candy day of the year, causing the company to report a 19 percent drop in third-quarter earnings that year.

The information system, which integrated components from SAP AG's R/3 applications suite, Siebel Systems, and Manugistics Group, was supposed to automate and modernize ordering and shipping for the candy company, which reports profits of over $4 billion a year. Installing this system was supposed to help Hershey's focus on its candy business after the company had sold off some of its tangential products to other manufacturers. The project included the installation of 5000 personal computers, network hubs, servers, and software designed to smooth every aspect of the company's production, distribution, and sale of candy. Despite the complexity of the system and the initial plan to install the system over a period of four years, Hershey stepped up the pace considerably to a 30-month plan, using the "big bang" approach to systems installation. In addition, the company ran at least three months behind schedule, with computers not even up and running until mid-July. While certainly the confusion of attempting to utilize three different systems together could have caused problems, industry

analysts best explain the fallout as a result of the overly undertaking should have been allowed the full four-year span to implement. While the company had expected to be fully functional in time for Christmas candies, the reality set in when system start-up problems lingered on past the first of the year. Retailers were forced to add to their orders from Mars and Nestle just to keep customers happy, and Hershey's was left with a stagnating inventory of Halloween goods well into bunny season.

Despite the presidential elections in the Fall of 2000, Halloween was less frightening for Hershey's, retailers, and trick-or-treaters. Hershey's reported a rise of 23 percent in profits over the previous year. The mere passage of time allowed the company to straighten out its problems with the ERP systems they had purchased in order to modernize the company. Hershey's also added that a revamped distribution facility on the East Coast helped significantly in the peak ordering period of the year. Lesson learned? Using a reasonable time frame to implement systems avoids major difficulties, although, well, your dentist might not argue if the candy trucks never did make it to market.

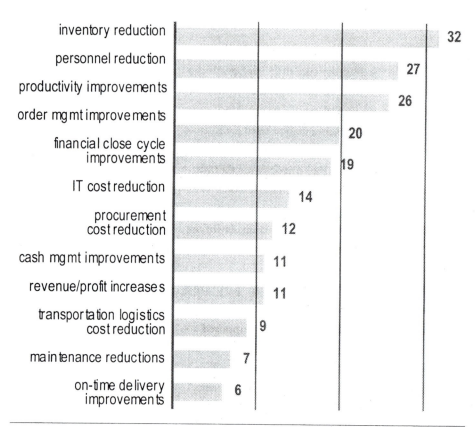

FIGURE 3-4. Tangible benefits (adapted from DC 99).

Process and technology-related obstacles, though less critical than people-related obstacles, are still significant and must be overcome to achieve successful integration of the enterprise. Poor management of the overall implementation program, inadequate reengineering of organizational processes, and clumsy or poorly planned transitions from one stage of enterprise system implementation to another are all examples of process-related obstacles. Inadequate functionality in the integrated systems, weaknesses in the portfolio of applications within the enterprise system, and difficulties with system enhancement or upgrading are examples of some of the major technology-related obstacles to enterprise integration.

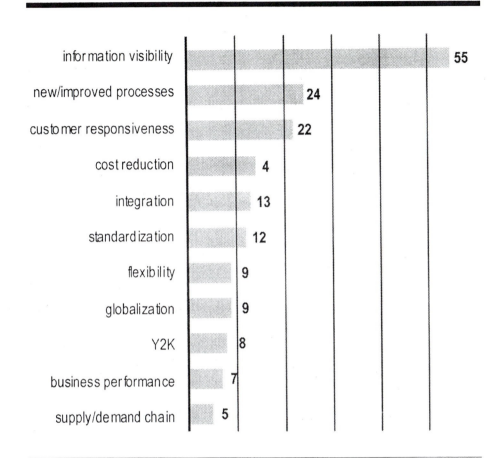

FIGURE 3-5. Intangible benefits (adapted from DC 99).

Actual Benefits of Integrated Systems

The actual benefits that an organization receives from its integration efforts are not necessarily congruent with the factors that motivated such efforts in the first place. Many of the benefits that an organization receives are tangible and can be easily measured in financial terms (see Figure 3-4). Other benefits to integration are intangible, but many are at least as important as the tangible benefits to the overall success of the organization (see Figure 3-5).

A QUANTUM LEAP: FROM PCS TO ERP IN A SINGLE BOUND

While industry analysts debate the wisdom of a "big bang" approach to system installation and implementation, one company has given credibility to an astronomical leap into the beyond. It's Quantum, another billion-dollar Silicon Valley computer manufacturer. For one week, Quantum shut down all operations; no ordering, no shipping, no money coming in or going out in any way so it could cut over from its old, outdated systems into a new ERP. After one week, the system proved fully operational, and it has been running smoothly ever since.

Quantum had been considering the big bang approach to implementation, despite its risks, since October 1992 but did not get under way with selecting its ERP partner Oracle until a year and a half later. With the acquisition of Digital Equipment Corporation's storage business in 1994, the need for a network of information systems was becoming more pronounced. Quantum decided to go with Oracle because it needed ATP (available-to-promise) ordering, and Oracle promised to deliver. And because of the way ATP works, giving the company the ability to take an order, schedule it for delivery, and confirm the transaction instantly, Quantum knew that it had to have the entire system functioning all at once. Company executives knew that it had to be a big bang. In fact, they justified it as being less risky than a phased approach. There was no other way into the universe of smooth, speedy marketing.

Dubbed WARP undoubtedly for its Trekkie, cola-pumped members, the Worldwide Ask Replacement Project team began its journey in the summer of 1994. At first, the team projected a date of summer 1995 for its leap, but system difficulties kept them from getting it off the ground that quickly. The team divided tasks through an organization chart, marking off those that were complete with a green, those that needed fine-tuning with yellow, and those that were real problems in red. When the chart showed mainly green lights, the company had the go-ahead to begin testing. After a couple of tests in the winter of 1996, the team saw that things were very close. So on April 26, 1996, Quantum shut down to begin the conversion from the old system to the new. The system did some test transactions. Everything worked. And on May 5 the big bang went off. Kaboom! Everything has been running smoothly since.

Such a successful big bang implementation causes some industry analysts to shake their heads in wonder. But looking at Quantum may give other companies ideas of how to do it right. One of the ways Quantum may have had such success with the big bang approach was the high level of user training. The company sponsored mandatory training for employees that lasted two to four weeks and required them to take a test at the end of this time before they could go back to their regular jobs. This meant that nobody was sitting at their desk on Mayday scratching their heads in confusion. Quantum also made a concerted effort to keep employee morale high during the arduous process of project implementation, even going so far as having company executives wash IS workers' automobiles.

Another speculation about its smooth transition to ERP is that Quantum did not make any heavy attempts to cut costs. While the company did not reveal exactly how much money it spent on updating its systems, it indicated that it was pretty expensive, as expensive as starting a whole new product line. It may have been this willingness to pay for extra details that really paid off in the end. Whatever the reasons, nobody seems to debate the choice to go head on into the wind as the new systems allow users to schedule orders, plan shipments, and confirm deliveries all in the blink of an eye. Quantum is happy to have made a big bang of its own in the galaxy of Silicon.

Foremost among tangible benefits is cost reduction, and the two areas that show the greatest benefit to the bottom line are the reduction of inventory costs and personnel costs. IT costs are also reduced but to a substantially smaller amount than is typically anticipated by those involved prior to the beginning of an integration effort. On the other hand, productivity gains are usually much larger than anticipated and are ranked among the greatest benefits to enterprise integration. The other major tangible area of benefit is the reduction of cycle times, particularly those associated with the processing and management of orders as well as financial processes such as period closings.

By far the largest intangible benefit to enterprise integration is the improved availability of information—information about the organization that is widely available throughout the organization. This increased "information visibility" that results from integrated information systems enables managers and senior executives to make informed decisions in a timely manner. Other intangible benefits to integration include the addition of new organizational processes and the improvement of existing ones, an increase in customer responsiveness, the establishment of enterprisewide standards for information resources, and the added flexibility that these standards provide.

Summary

In this chapter, we presented the challenge of integrating information systems in large modern enterprises. We began with an exploration of some of the more common motivations for integration. Next, we outlined the obstacles that companies embarking on such integration efforts are likely to face, with an emphasis on people, process, and technology-related obstacles. Then, we described some of the tangible and intangible benefits of integration that organizations actually achieve through integration of their information systems. The chapter concluded with a presentation of two industry examples of success and failure in enterprise integration.

Discussion Questions

1. Distinguish between an organization's operational and technical motivation to integrate its information systems. Describe a situation where either operational or technical motivation is likely to dominate the decision to integrate.

2. What is the relationship between motivation to integrate an enterprise and actual benefits to integration? In what areas are motivation and benefits congruent and where are they divergent?

3. What do the authors mean by "information visibility?" How does enterprise integration lead to greater visibility for managers and executives?

4. What were some of the major causes of the enterprise integration fiasco at Hershey? How could problems have been avoided? In what ways did Quantum succeed at implementation where Hershey failed? What important lessons can be learned from these two efforts at enterprise integration?

References

Branch, Shelly. "Hershey's Net Sinks by 19%; Snafus Linger." *The Wall Street Journal,* October 26, 1999.

Branch, Shelly. "Hershey's Will Miss Earnings Estimates by as Much as 10%." *The Wall Street Journal,* September 14, 1999.

Deloitte Consulting. *ERP's Second Wave: Maximizing the Value of ERP-Enabled Processes.* 1999.

Nelson, Emily and Evan Ramstad. "Kiss Your Hershey Treats Goodbye." *The Wall Street Journal,* October 29, 1999.

Radosevich, Lynda. "Quantum's Leap: One Computer Manufacturer's Risky Decision to Overhaul Its Worldwide Business Systems in a Single Bound Paid Off." *CIO Magazine,* February 15, 1997.

Songini, Marc. "Halloween Less Haunting for Hershey's This Year." *Computer World Magazine,* November 2, 2000.

Stedman, Craig. "Failed ERP Gamble Haunts Hershey." *Computer World Magazine,* November 1, 1999.

A New Environment for Enterprise Systems

I n this part, enterprise systems are examined in terms of some of their most fundamental components. These components include organizational processes, distributed information technologies, and database management systems. Part Two concludes with a chapter that describes how these components are combined in a typical architecture of an enterprise system.

Chapter 4

Let's Get Horizontal: Toward a Process View of Organization

Hell hath no fury like a bureaucrat scorned. — Milton Friedman

Until recently, most organizations were comprised of units that were based on business functions. And as a basis of organizing, it worked okay. That is, it worked fine just as long as not much changed, competition remained mild, and customers kept coming in the doors. But times have changed. Competition in most areas has become intense, and instead of coming through physical doors, customers are expecting to enter through the virtual doors of organizational web sites.

One of the most promising ways for organizations to reinvent themselves is to focus on processes rather than functions. This new view means turning the organization

---

OBJECTIVES

♦ Explore organizational motivations for enterprise integration

♦ Understand common obstacle to integration

♦ Identify tangible and intangible benefits to integration

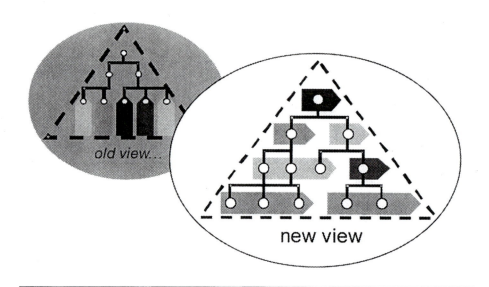

FIGURE 4-1. Moving from a functional to a process view of organization.

on its side—concentrating on those activities that cut horizontally across an organization's traditional functional areas (see Figure 4.1).

This chapter begins by discussing the composition of organizational units. The two most common ways of grouping—grouping by function and grouping by process—are introduced and compared. Next, business processes are defined and examined in detail in terms of their granularity, relative advantages, and cross-functional nature. The chapter concludes with a case study of an organization that is highly successful and is organized by process.

Making Parts into Wholes: The Composition of Organizational Units

In Chapter 2, we discussed the stages of growth of organizations and the necessary changes to their mechanisms for coordination and control. Mutual adjustment only works well at a very small scale and is soon replaced by direct supervision that gradually gives way to various forms of standardization practices as an organization increases in size and complexity. At the same time that coordination and control mechanisms are changing, another fundamental change occurs within organizations as they grow. Immediately upon moving away from mutual adjustment, whereby all members of the organization are in direct communication with all others, individuals and their work must be arranged into groups. A key factor in organizational design is deciding exactly how and on what basis to form these groups.

Grouping by Function

One way to group individuals is to organize them into units according to the type of work that they do or according to their knowledge or skills. This functional basis of grouping is most useful when the kind of work being done is highly interdependent—each person's work is closely related and interwoven with that of their co-workers. Grouping by function also makes sense when economies of scale can be achieved, such as having a centralized service or facility that performs better than or could not otherwise be justified in a distributed setting. For example, a centralized maintenance department might serve half a dozen organizational units with three people, whereas six workers would be required if this function were decentralized.

Organizing by function makes it easier to add new employees because the scope of their immediate learning is limited to the particular functional area. Not only is indoctrination faster and easier, but also because of the high degree of specialization, the development of expertise can be fostered within functional groups. Functional grouping has many social benefits, including greater camaraderie among like-minded people.

On the other hand, functionally organized groups are often parochial—with little more than a narrow perspective on organizational goals or purpose. In part because of this limitation, they lack built-in objectives that directly relate to organizational goals and could otherwise serve as mechanisms for coordination of their activities. As such, functional organizations have an extra need for coordination and control from above, which tends to result in a more formalized or bureaucratic structure.

As discussed in Chapter 2, the functionally structured organization is the most common form of organization today. Large, global, diversified firms that often have some other basis for organizing their upper levels—such as geographic region, product group, or customer base—are commonly organized along functional lines at lower levels. Standard functional areas include: finance, operations, marketing, engineering, human resources, sales and distribution, and information systems.

Grouping by Process

An alternative way of grouping individuals and their activities is based on business processes that cut horizontally across traditional functional areas. This process-oriented basis of grouping is most appropriate when there are significant interdependencies across the entire workflow. This often occurs in manufacturing contexts where, for example, a particular process might consist of a series of interlocking steps.

The most significant advantage of organizing by process is that it promotes a sense of territorial integrity or ownership among the workers or participants in the processes involved. This is because well-defined processes represent "psychologically complete tasks." Because the sequencing of activities is a strong feature of processes, this often acts as a built-in mechanism for coordinating work. According to Davenport (2000), a process is a "structure for action," and the existence of this structure reduces the requirement for hierarchical supervision or control. Furthermore, with a predefined set of inputs and outputs, performance of a process is easy to determine. Not only are processes measurable, but also they are also easier to improve.

On the other hand, organizing around processes is often more wasteful of resources when compared with the economies of scale in personnel and facilities that functional grouping can achieve. The result can be a duplication of people and equipment. Another disadvantage of process grouping is a general lack of interaction across individuals who share similar professional backgrounds, education, or specialized training. This may diminish the sense of professional worth of skilled workers and potentially lower the overall quality of the work that they perform.

Comparing Functional and Process-oriented Groupings

It is possible to compare functions and processes in terms of their role as building blocks of organizations according to their primary focus, organizational orientation, main objective, use of personnel, and perspective within the firm. Table 4-1 summarizes this comparison.

Dimension	Functions	Processes
Primary focus	"what"; static; slice-in-time	"how"; dynamic
Organizational orientation	vertical; chain of command	horizontal; workflow
Objective	task-centered	customer-oriented
Personnel	individual specialists	teams of generalists
Perspective	parochial	holistic

TABLE 4-1. Functions versus processes.

Business Processes

In Chapter 1, we quoted Davenport's definition of a business process as "a specific ordering of work activities across time and place, with a beginning, an end, and clearly identified inputs and outputs." Three important characteristics implicit in this definition are that processes are a sequence of activities, have an end or purpose, and involve some level of interaction.

The preceding definition of business process is vague about the level of granularity or scale of processes. Obviously, we can define processes as complex organizational phenomena that involve innumerable steps, hundreds of people, and a great deal of time to complete. At the other extreme, a process could consist of those activities associated with an individual person stapling two pieces of paper together. It is perhaps more useful to think of processes in terms that are closer to the first example. In fact, when asked to identify their fundamental business processes, most organizations—ranging from very large to quite small—list about 20 or less. Some examples of typical business processes are shown in Table 4-2.

Advantages of Business Process Orientation

A number of factors underscore a process orientation within any organization. First, a focus on processes automatically encourages a greater focus on customers. At one level, the "customers" of a process may be

Business Process

Product development

Customer relationship management

Operations/manufacturing

Order processing

Human resource management

Investment management

Plant and equipment maintenance

Construction and project management

Planning & resource allocation

TABLE 4-2. Typical business processes.

individuals, units, or other processes within the firm; in a broader sense, the orientation of all processes within the organization is inherently focused on the true end customer of its products and/or services. Processes have clearly defined owners—usually the individuals whose activities comprise them—who are responsible for driving the process forward, setting performance standards, and ensuring the satisfactory generation of outputs. They can do this because processes are highly measurable in terms that directly relate to organizational goals, such as usefulness, consistency, variability, and quality. Ultimately, a process orientation provides a dynamic view of how an organization delivers value that can become a basis for improving how work is done. Process design, improvement, and innovation are discussed in greater detail in Chapter 9.

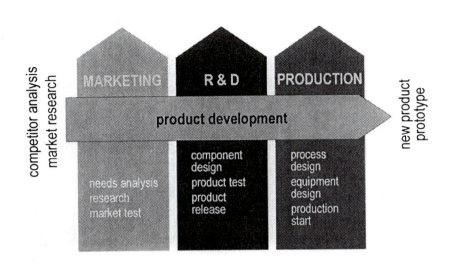

FIGURE 4-2. Cross-functional processes: product development.

Cross-Functional Processes

Most major organizational processes are cross-functional—that is, they span multiple functional areas of the enterprise. In some cases, this spanning is purely sequential, where the work is completed in one functional area before being passed on to the next. However, in most cases, cross-functional processes involve reciprocal or simultaneous interactions between two or more functional areas. Reciprocal activity occurs where the work flows repeatedly back and forth between functional areas until it is completed or passed on to another area. Simultaneous interactions occur when the multiple inputs are needed at the same time from different functional areas.

One example of a cross-functional process is new product development. At a minimum, this process involves inputs from traditional functional areas that include marketing, research and development (or engineering), and production (or operations) as the work progresses from an analysis of the market to the development of a prototype. Marketing activities include needs assessment, market research, and market testing. Research and development activities include component design, product testing, and

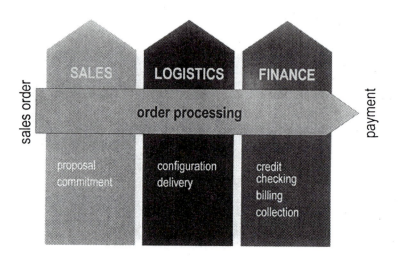

FIGURE 4-3. Cross-functional processes: order processing.

product release. Production activities include design of the production process, equipment design, and commencing production (see Figure 4-2).

Although some of the workflow in product development is sequential, many activities are interdependent. For example, most of the activities between research and development and production are reciprocal—product testing must occur before the start of production, but product release usually occurs later. Some of the activities are clearly simultaneous as well. Component design, for example, is an activity that typically requires input from both marketing and research and development.

Another example of cross-functional process is order processing. At a minimum, this process involves inputs from traditional functional areas that include sales, logistics, and finance as the work progresses from the initial sales order to the collection of payment from the customer. Sales activities include the original sales proposal and the commitment from the customer (usually in the form of a sales order). Logistics activities include configuration and delivery. Finance activities include credit checking, billing, and payment collection (see Figure 4-3).

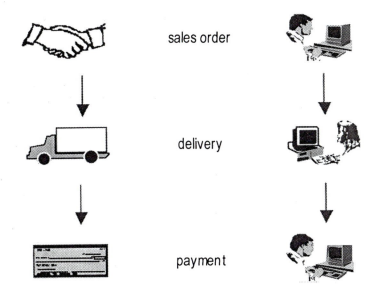

sales order

delivery

payment

FIGURE 4-4. Order processing: phycial, logial, and information flows.

Here again, because of the interdependent nature of order processing, we have sequential, reciprocal, and simultaneous activities occurring in the workflow. An example of reciprocal activities is that credit checking by the finance area will usually occur before the order is delivered, which must occur before billing the customer and collecting payment.

If we examine the order processing process a bit further, we see that the information flows parallel both the physical and logical workflows (see Figure 4-4).

The fact that most business processes have parallel physical, logical, and information flows is very useful because it makes it relatively easy to design and build integrated information systems to support such processes. Unlike information systems that are based on specific functional areas of

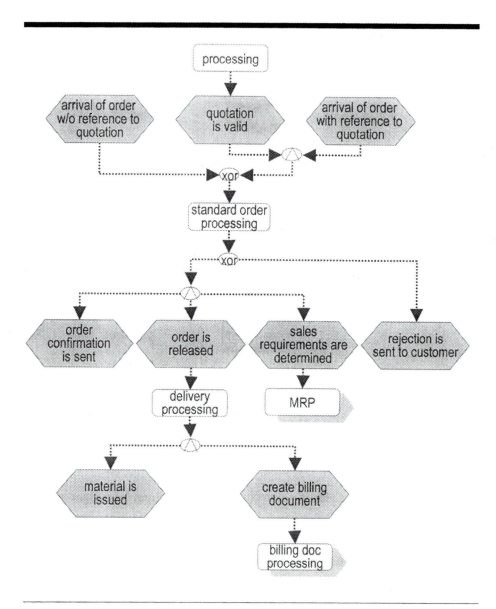

FIGURE 4-5. Logical model of order processing.

the enterprise, a process-oriented viewpoint fosters integration. Figure 4-5 is an example of a model that is based on order processing as described above. Such models are used in the construction of information systems and are described in greater detail in Chapter 9.

CISCO'S CHALLENGE: ERP IMPLEMENTATION IN JUST 15 MONTHS

Cisco Systems Inc., the Silicon Valley-based company whose primary product is routers, was started in 1990 by two computer scientists. Today Cisco boasts annual revenues of more than $8 billion, and a market capitalization of over $100 billion. The company alone accounted for more than one-third of all electronic commerce in 2000. Although Cisco's success has been attributed to its CEO John Chambers and his ardent focus on the customer, as well as its strategic acquisitions of other companies, Cisco can also attribute its smooth sailing to the top of the e-commerce world to its successful big-bang implementation of ERP.

While deciding on, building, and implementing an ERP system successfully in just 15 months may sound like those ads promising you can lose 10 pounds in time for your cousin's wedding, Cisco proved it could be done. Early in 1993, Pete Solvik joined Cisco as the company's new CIO. He knew the company needed a major technological overhaul but was unsure what direction to take in doing so. After Cisco went through a series of technological mini-crises in early 1994, he knew the company had to act fast. A team was formed to choose a vendor for an ERP system. Cisco was concerned that the team choose a vendor who wasn't smaller than they were. After two and a half months of discussion, proposals, and demonstrations, they settled on Oracle.

After reviewing time lines and budgets for the project, they recommended to Cisco's board of directors that the ERP solution for Cisco's technological needs be implemented big-bang style, giving a start-to-finish date for the entire project in nine months (at a mere $15 million

for the entire thing!). It was to be the single largest capital project ever approved by the company.

The core team expanded and subdivided, with each sub-team being given a task. In order to offer training to the members of the teams, Cisco directed Oracle to compress its training sessions so that team members would be "immersed" in the new technology. While the company initially wanted to avoid any major modifications to the ERP software, they ended up having to make some substantial changes to fill in gaps in the system where the ERP software could not totally support the necessary business processes.

Finally, in February 1995, Cisco was ready cut over to Oracle. At first, there were some major glitches, with the system going down at least once a day. Pete Solvik noted that the on-time ship date for customers had gone from 95 percent to 75 percent with the cutover. Problems were not only isolated in the software realm, where the software had not been tested on a large enough database and therefore lacked the capacity to process the required amount of transactions, but in the area of hardware as well, where sizing also proved to be a difficulty. However, Cisco's problems with its transition to ERP proved to be short-lived, and within three months after implementation it was able to function normally. Celebration ensued, and guess what? The ERP team received a whopping $200,000 bonus for the deal.

Business Process Reengineering

Over the years the process known as BPR (Business Process Reengineering—see Hammer and Champy, 1993—or Business Process Redesign) has taken on many meanings. The acronym was first used by Michael Hammer as a solution to the cumbersome processes that were in place in many American firms during the 1980s. In his famous 1990 article called "Reengineering Work: Don't Automate, Obliterate," he encouraged organizations to take a hard look at themselves and the processes that ran their businesses for years and to question why things were done the way they were. He encouraged firms to streamline processes and get rid of unnecessary steps and to reengineer the organization from the top down. For this reason, the BPR movement of the early 1990s became synonymous with downsizing.

The truth is that many of the concepts that underlie BPR have been around for several years and that BPR is similar to other movements designed to improve business processes such as Quality Function Deployment, Quality Circles, Continuous Improvement, and the House of Quality. Movement towards a quality approach measured in the eyes of the customer can be traced back to the work of W.E. Deming in his book *Out of the Crisis* (1986). He listed 14 points that organizations needed to use to help organizations become more productive and customer focused. Among these points were constant improvement, empowering workers, and creating environments that improve the processes for both workers and management.

Michael Hammer (1990, 1993) took the idea of transformation from the department or single-process level to the level of the whole organization. Reengineering was meant to introduce radical change or a paradigm shift within the organization and to question everything. Thus, the main difference between a quality circle that is at the lowest level of granularity of a process and reengineering which is the broadest possible context is the degree to which the proposed changes reach into all levels of the organization.

The principles of reengineering adapted from Hammer (1990) include the following:

1. Organize around outcomes (not tasks). In other words, have one person do all the tasks that lead to one outcome.

2. Have those who use the output of a process perform the tasks that produce the output.

3. Subsume any information processing work (or tasks) into the real work of the process. (In other words, don't have tasks that just put data into an information system or transcribe data from one system to another.)

4. Treat geographically dispersed resources as though they were centralized by having databases and networks get information into the hands of all those who need it.

5. Link parallel activities instead of integrating their results.

6. Put the decision point at the place where work is performed and build any needed controls into the work process, instead of having levels of decisionmaking and control outside of the real work process.

7. Capture information one time, one place, at the source.

8. Look at the process from the customer's perspective and eliminate anything that does not add value to the customer. (Note that customers of processes can be internal or external.) Stakeholder is also appropriate here.

9. Steps in the process need to be performed in a natural order. (Eliminate handoffs and straight-line sequencing.)

10. Use a balanced approach to checks and balances. (Know the economic value of every checkpoint.)

11. Minimize reconciliation tasks.

Summary

This chapter began with a discussion of how organizational units are composed. We introduced and compared the two most common ways of grouping—grouping by function and grouping by process. Then, business processes were defined and examined in detail in terms of their granularity, relative advantages, and cross-functional nature. The chapter concluded with a case study of an organization that is highly successful and is organized by process.

Discussion Questions

1. What are some major advantages and disadvantages of a functional versus a process grouping of work? Can you think of any situation where functional grouping is ideal? Where does process grouping work best?

2. Think of a cross-functional business process. (If possible, choose one that you are familiar with from work, school, or an organization to which you belong.) Identify all the functional areas that the process touches. What information passes from one area to the next? Is the process purely sequential? Or does it involve reciprocal or simultaneous interactions?

3. Business Process Reengineering offers many positive benefits to organizations. But there is a dark side to reengineering. What are some of the negative consequences of business process reengineering? for organizations? for employees? for society?

4. What difficulties did Cisco encounter during its rapid implementation of its ERP system? How could they have been avoided?

References

"The Corporation of the Future." *Business Week,* August 31, 1998.

Cotteleer, Mark, Robert Austen, and Richard Nolan. "Cisco Systems, Inc.: Implementing ERP," Case 9-699-022. Boston: Harvard Business School Press, 1998.

Davenport, Thomas H. *Mission Critical: Realizing the Promise of Enterprise Systems.* Boston: Harvard Business School Press, 2000.

Deming, W.E. *Out of the Crisis.* Cambridge, Mass.: MIT Press, 1986.

Hammer, Michael. "Reengineering Work: Don't Automate, Obliterate." *Harvard Business Review* 68(1990): 104–111.

Hammer, Michael, and James Champy. *Reengineering the Corporation.* New York: Harper Business Press, 1993.

Mintzberg, Henry. *The Structuring of Organizations.* Englewood Cliffs, N.J.: Prentice-
   Hall, 1979.

Chapter 5

The Relentless Distribution of Information Technology

Technological progress is like an axe in the hands of a pathological criminal. — Albert Einstein

The prevailing wisdom a decade ago was that the evolution of information systems was marked by cycles. The most significant cycle, according to academics and industry pundits alike, was prescribed by the pendulum that swung between the order of centralized computing and decentralized chaos. As information technology became increasingly distributed, there was always something on the horizon that hinted at the return of centralized control of IT.

But the reality is becoming clearer every day: it's not cyclical. The pendulum is never coming back! Instead, IS managers are facing a relentless march toward ever increasing levels of distribution. Although scary for some, this is not necessarily a bad prospect. There are

---

---

many technical and managerial strategies that people in charge of corporate information systems can use to bring order to distributed systems.

The chapter begins by discussing the evolution of corporate networks from the early days of LANs and WANs to their modern counterparts: the Internet, intranets, and extranets. Next, we introduce you to three critical challenges that managers are likely to face when deploying distributed information systems, and in the following section, we present some managerial solutions and technical approaches to these challenges. In the final section on architecture and strategy, client-server architecture is defined in terms of its three tiers: presentation, business logic, and data; in addition, the importance of developing an enterprise information architecture is discussed.

Getting Wired: The Evolution of Corporate Networks

In Chapter 2, we discussed the eras of information technology management. As IT management moved from the second to the third era, the proliferation of PCs created a strong impetus to connect them together into networks. Although networks of computers had existed for decades before the PC, the sheer number of computational devices that existed soon after the introduction of the PC brought issues of connectivity to the forefront and made networking one of the most important issues of the preceding 20 years.

The drive to combine small groups of PCs into networks came from two organizational constituencies that did not see eye to eye on many things: IT management and the end-user community. To end users, the PC was a tool that liberated them from their dependence on the often bureaucratic and centralized information systems department. They viewed networking as a way to increase the capabilities of their individual desktop computers by allowing them to access corporate data resources. To the information systems professionals, the PC was at best a headache and often a threat to their established power base. They saw networking as a way to regain control of corporate computing while reducing the fragmentation of IT resources that the proliferation of PCs appeared to be causing. Networking represented the classic win-win scenario in most organizations and thus became a popular and viable option throughout the business world.

LANs and WANs

Throughout the 1980s, networks of PCs known as Local Area Networks or LANs became a widespread and increasingly important computing platform in organizations of all sizes. Initially, LANs consisted of a small collection of PCs called workstations that connected to a typically more powerful PC called a file server. Toward the end of the 1980s, the size and sophistication of corporate LANs had grown substantially, and a new term emerged to refer to this phenomenon: client-server computing.

At the same time as LANs were revolutionizing corporate information systems on the inside, a parallel but older tradition known as Wide Area Networks or WANs was allowing organizations that were geographically dispersed to connect their information resources together. In addition, companies were also attempting to extend their networks to connect to suppliers and customers in what were known as interorganizational information systems. But WANs were always an order of magnitude slower than LANs and much more complex to deploy and maintain. One of the most significant challenges to these extended corporate networks was the large number of inconsistent and incompatible communications protocols. (A protocol is a set of rules that establishes exactly how information is to be exchanged from one system to another, and if two systems use different protocols, they cannot communicate.)

The Internet, Intranets, and Extranets

By the beginning of the 1990s, a new global phenomenon was gaining popularity and recognition as a possible answer to the problem of incompatible protocols. It was called the Internet. Even before the invention of the World Wide Web, the protocol suite that supported the Internet called Transmission Control Protocol/Internet Protocol (TCP/IP) was seen as extremely simple and relatively universal, and thus became widely adopted as the preferred networking platform for global computing.

The dominance of the Internet became unambiguous with the emergence and immediate popularity of the World Wide Web in the mid-1990s. With the creation of the web, TCP/IP became the de facto standard for public networks. It was logical, therefore, to extend this standard both internally and interorganizationally. So, as firms have applied TCP/IP to their internal networks, these have become known as intranets. An intranet is often described as the Internet brought inside the organization. It is important to note that, in most organizations, this did not mean adding another network to the existing LANs or client-server networks. Usually, creating an intranet for a company involves the simple and behind-the-scenes step of turning on preexisting TCP/IP connections. But for most employees, an intranet becomes visible and is best known for the web-based applications that run on their companies' networks.

Just as the internal application of TCP/IP became known as intranets, the external application of TCP/IP has recently been dubbed the extranet. This begs the question: How is an extranet different from a WAN? The fact is that there is more of a difference between an extranet and a WAN than between an intranet and a LAN. Like an intranet, an extranet uses TCP/IP. But unlike intranets and LANs, extranets rarely use the same network infrastructure that supports WANs. In a WAN, connections between geographically dispersed units of an organization, or between the organization and its partners, were usually created through the use of leased or purchased lines provided by private telecommunications companies. An extranet makes these same connections by creating a secure channel over the public infrastructure of the Internet. These secure channels are known as virtual private networks, and they provide the same functionality as old-style WANs at a fraction of the cost.

More than an evolution of technology, it sometimes appears that we have witnessed an evolution of terminology over the past two decades. Clearly, the terms LAN and WAN have been largely replaced by intranet and extranet, respectively. But this change of terms does reflect a couple of fundamental changes in the makeup of corporate computing networks. These changes include the emergence of a standard for networking, TCP/IP, and the increasing reliance on the use of a common and public network infrastructure, the Internet. Although this opens the door on a world of possibilities, it also requires substantial effort to handle the managerial and technical challenges of distributed systems.

Distribution and Control

The central problem in managing the information systems function within organizations today is how to most effectively deliver services and provide access to resources in a distributed computing environment while at the same time maintaining control of those resources. People who manage the IT resources of organizations struggle daily with this problem. The problem itself breaks down into three broad managerial challenges associated with connectivity, availability, and performance.

Connectivity

Connectivity is the ability of computer systems to connect to networks and exchange information with other computers on those networks. If all computer systems were identical, including their hardware, operating systems, and applications, connectivity would be simple. But connectivity becomes a major challenge in the face of the wide diversity of computing platforms and networks present in most organizations as well as the increasing geographic dispersal of users and systems that results from an increasingly globalized and mobilized workforce.

Availability

When you plug an appliance into an outlet, you rarely question whether consistent power will be available. Similarly, when you pick up the telephone, you expect a dial tone. Availability for information systems means that whenever end users connect, they are able to access the services and resources that they need at the time. Organizational information systems begin to be viewed much like utilities, and the expectation is that upon connecting to the network, an "information dial tone" will be provided around the clock. The challenge for IS managers is to maximize availability in the face of relatively fragile computing platforms and networking technologies.

Performance

Performance of an information system is a moving target. To a large extent, performance is dependent on the expectations of the users of a particular information system. Thirty years ago, it was acceptable and normal for a filing clerk to take several hours or even days to locate a requested piece of information from a warehouse containing rows of file cabinets. Today, users are infuriated with a three-minute delay in the retrieval of the equivalent information from an electronic filing system supported by the latest

User Requirement	IS Management Strategy	Technical Approaches
Connectivity	Build transparent solutions	Standards, directories, security
Availability	Build reliable solutions	Redundancy, monitoring, isolation
Performance	Build scalable solutions	Server specialization, load balancing

TABLE 5-1. Management strategies for distributed IT.

database technology. Not only are the expectations of users putting additional demands on information system performance, but also the sheer volume of users is increasing dramatically in most organizations. Maintaining an acceptable level of performance in the face of both increasing demand and increasing expectations is one more significant management challenge.

Building a Distributed Infrastructure

As end-user requirements for connectivity, availability, and performance continue to challenge information systems management, a number of generic strategies and specific technical solutions have emerged in recent years. The challenge of connectivity is met through building transparent solutions that depend on the application of standards, directory services, and security. Building reliable solutions through redundancy, system monitoring, and component isolation is a strategy applied to the challenge of availability. The challenge of performance is met by building scalable solutions that rely on server specialization and load balancing. These management strategies and technical solutions are summarized in Table 5-1.

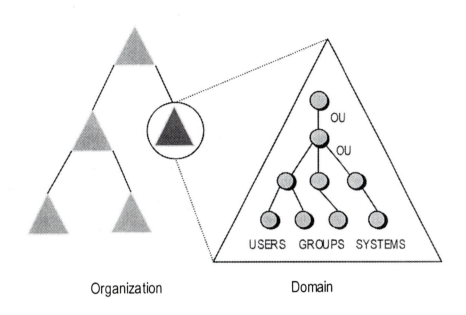

Organization   Domain

FIGURE 5-1. Directory services.

Building Transparent Solutions

The strategy that IS management employs to achieve the connectivity that users require is to provide transparent access to IT services and resources. Transparency can be achieved through the application of standards, the deployment of directory services, and the use of security.

Standards

Most IS managers face a heterogeneous computing environment and, in these cases, transparency can be realized through the establishment and enforcement of standards. For example, a company can specify that all desktop systems use a particular operating system and that all database servers operate on the same platform. More important is for an organization to establish standards for its networks. Most intranets achieve a high degree of transparency by leveraging the common platform of the web browser for consistent access to information resources across widely diverse desktop operating systems.

Directory Services

Another technical solution toward creating transparent access to resources is to provide enterprisewide directory services (Figure 5-1). By directory, we mean any comprehensive catalog of IT resources and services, users and roles, security information, and so on. Directory services typically utilize a hierarchical structure that permits storage, search, and access to enterprise resources. In terms of transparency, directory services allow users and systems to access these resources without having to know anything about their physical location.

Security

Although directory services can permit users to access resources throughout the enterprise, it is obvious that access should rarely be unlimited. So the essential counterpart to directory services is security services. Whereas directory services provide transparency, security services provide the necessary opacity in terms of access to IT resources. The result is that users see what they need to see and have access to those resources that they need to access. There are many forms of security, but the most successful strategy today involves three levels: users, roles, and resources. In this model, roles are assigned to specific resources, and then users are assigned to specific roles. As a user's job changes, they can be added to or subtracted from roles. Users and resources can have multiple roles, and roles can be assigned to multiple resources and users. For example, a user may be an accounts payable clerk allowing a specific kind of access to the accounts payable information system. The same user may also be part of a purchasing department with access to certain functions in the procurement system.

Building Reliable Solutions

To achieve the kind of availability that most users have come to expect from their information systems, designers of these systems strive to maximize the reliability of these systems. To a large degree, this is an engineering problem, and the makers of computer and network hardware and software

are continually improving the reliability of these systems. But keeping pace with the increased reliability of information technologies are the increased expectations of users for highly available systems. And no matter how well engineered a system is, failures still occur. The question is: are there effective strategies that can be used when deploying systems within organizations that will minimize the impact of failures and maximize the availability of these systems to the end users?

Redundancy

The most common and dependable way to ensure reliability is to build redundancy into a system. This means duplicating a sensitive or critical element of an information system so that if there is a failure of that element, a spare part is readily available. The goal is to incorporate redundancy wherever it is appropriate, technically feasible, and cost-effective. Although most automobiles carry a spare tire, they don't typically carry a spare engine; it is neither cost-effective to provide a second engine nor realistic to expect a motorist to change an automobile's engine on the side of some busy highway.

A *fault-tolerant* system is one that not only incorporates redundancy, but at the same time provides a mechanism for redirecting access or processing in the event of a failure in the working resource. This mechanism is referred to as *failover*. The goal is to minimize **downtime** and data loss by providing as close to instantaneous failover as possible. This usually requires some type of continual or periodic monitoring of the sensitive resource.

Redundancy can be applied to many different parts of an information system. One common form of fault-tolerant system that is applied to mass storage systems is called a redundant array of inexpensive disks or RAID. Although there are several levels of RAID, almost all incorporate some form of mirroring or duplicating data across a series of disk drives such that a single drive failure will cause no loss of data and no system downtime. In another kind of fault-tolerant solution, the entire system, not just the storage media, is duplicated so that every transaction is simultaneously recorded through both systems. The chances of both systems failing at the exact same time are astronomical.

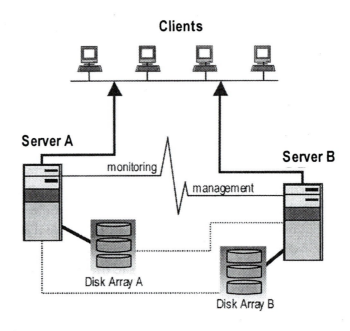

FIGURE 5-2. Fault tolerance through isolation and monitoring.

Isolation

An alternative strategy for creating robust solutions is to isolate vulnerable components of a system from one another and provide multiple access routes to the components (Figure 5-2). An example of this strategy involves the separation of disk arrays from system processors. In the event a processor fails, another system that has been monitoring that processor's "heartbeat" can assume control of the disk array that is normally assigned to the failed processor.

Building Scalable Solutions

Poor performance of an information system is highly subjective—it depends on the application being used and the people using it. There are, however, a couple of commonly used, objective measures of performance: throughput and response time. Throughput is the volume of transactions that can be processed in a given unit of time. Response time is the length of time from a user's request for information to the return of information to the user. Clearly, a user's expectations can determine whether or not a given response time is an acceptable level of performance.

Although there are many technical causes of performance problems, the underlying cause of most situations is a lack of resources in one or more parts of the system. Bottlenecks may occur in many places within a system—lack of memory, insufficient processor capacity, and network latency caused by distance or congestion are all frequent problems. The common thread is that, in slow systems, there are one or more points that are not sufficiently scaled to handle the processing demands that users put on the system.

Rarely are bottlenecks intentionally designed into a system. Bottlenecks typically arise from an unforeseeable or unanticipated increase in demand for resources. A poor strategy that attempts to cope with such growth is to build huge reserves of excess capacity into every part of a system. This strategy usually fails in one of two ways: either the reserves in some part of the system are still insufficient and bottlenecks emerge, or the person who executes this strategy is removed for fiscal irresponsibility.

A more effective strategy is to design scalable systems. Although it is never possible to anticipate every area in which growth may occur or every impact that growth may have on a system, it is possible to design systems that can grow as demand increases. Many strategies can be employed to achieve scalability. Among the most successful are the specialization of services and the use of load balancing techniques.

Specialization of Services

Just as the division of labor is an effective strategy for managing problems of scale and complexity in human organizations, dividing computing services into focused roles is one of the best ways to achieve scalability of an information system. Specialization improves scalability in two ways. First, it allows a set of IT resources to be optimized for their particular tasks. For example, a set of IT resources that is dedicated to providing communications services can be designed and built for that purpose. Second, specialization allows a hierarchy of resources to be created, allowing computing services to be broken down and delivered in parallel rather than linear fashion.

A number of well-established techniques have been developed to accommodate the specialization of servers in a distributed computing environment. The simplest and most generic type of server is a file server. File servers have been around since the earliest LANs, and they serve clients by delivering requested files of any type. Print servers coordinate network printing activities, and manage the spooling and allocation of print jobs to the various printer resources on the network. Database servers provide a greater degree of specialization than file servers because they deliver only requested datasets in response to client queries instead of entire files.

In recent years, a number of newer approaches have been employed in the specialization of services provided across networks. Application servers, also known as transaction or component servers, broker client requests for processing and data access. Groupware servers, such as Lotus Notes, provide integrated data services aimed at supporting collaboration across networks. Finally, web servers have become an important feature of organizational networks for the dissemination of internal as well as external information.

OLTP versus OLAP

One very successful specialization strategy is to divide all requests for services into two major groups: those involving the routine and immediate processing of transaction data (known as online transaction processing or OLTP) and those involving the ad hoc, historical analysis of data (referred to as online analytic processing or OLAP). Since these types of requests put very different demands on information systems and networks, directing client requests to the appropriate OLTP or OLAP server is a proven strategy for improving performance.

Load Balancing

Another way to achieve scalability in a distributed information system is to perform some form of load balancing. Load balancing, a mechanism that is deployed via hardware, software, or both, aims to divide the workload generated by user requests in a balanced way across the available server resources.

The simplest way to achieve load balancing is to maintain a list of all available servers and then pass incoming requests to each server in turn in round-robin fashion. In a situation where all requests are roughly equivalent in terms of the load they put on the system and where all servers are approximately as powerful, then this simple form of load balancing works pretty well. However, homogeneity, in terms of both requests and server capabilities, is actually quite rare, and so more sophisticated approaches are often employed.

In the next level of load balancing, the server that is handling all incoming traffic, often called a dispatcher, monitors the performance of each server to which it passes requests and, using complex algorithms, assigns future requests accordingly. These load balancing algorithms can take into account each server's history of performance across various kinds of transactions, the priority of each request, and so on.

Load balancing is almost always transparent to the end user. In other words, the client views a cluster of servers as a single resource and does not care, or indeed is not even aware of, which server is handling its request. In most cases, this works fine, but at times it is important for a client to continue to access the same server throughout a computing session. One reason for this could be that, to enhance performance, a server will often store a large quantity of information in a cache while only returning the data of immediate interest to the client across the network. Subsequent requests for related data can be pulled from the cache without having to wait for the upstream database server to process an additional request. The advantages of caching can be realized only if the dispatcher always directs the client to the same server. Such capability is called *affinity* and is common in the most sophisticated load balancing systems.

Finally, load balancing is not limited to interactions between clients and servers. Any place in a network where work is being performed by multiple servers or *clusters* is a candidate for load balancing. Load balancing often occurs between a server of one kind and a cluster of servers of another kind. In the following section, we talk about the use of tiers in distributed computing. It is becoming increasingly commonplace for each tier in a client-server system to utilize load balancing across the servers within that tier.

Architecture and Strategy

The earliest attempts to define an architecture for distributed computing divided the processing into two tiers: client and server. Hence, the original

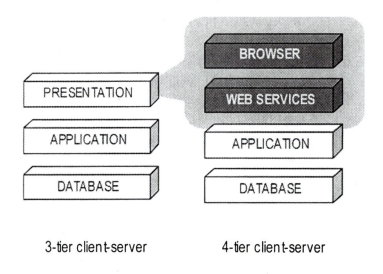

3-tier client-server   4-tier client-server

FIGURE 5-3. Dividing presentation services in a web application.

---

term for distributed computing is client-server computing or client-server architecture. As the technology of distributed computing advanced, practitioners soon discovered that a two-tier architecture was not adequate in terms of performance and growth—it was not scalable.

Three-Tier Client-Server Architecture

Enter three-tier client-server computing. Regardless of the strategy for dividing the services among tiers (more on this later), simply adding another layer of services enhances the overall scalability of the architecture. For example, suppose your average server can handle 100 active users at any time. In a two-tier architecture, you'll be limited to just that–100 users. Now imagine keeping the same server specifications but adding an intermediate layer of servers such that all clients communicate with an intermediate server and the intermediate server passes on their requests to a single top-level server. Suddenly, your upward limit is 10,000 active users. That's a pretty significant jump in scalability.

The classic three-tier client-server architecture divides the services that are provided to its users among three tiers: the presentation tier, the business

---

logic tier, and the data tier. Each of these tiers has a specialized function that is described in the sections that follow. But first, it is important to understand that the three-tier client-server architecture is merely a model for dividing up the processing within an information system. When implemented, client-server systems often support more than three tiers. In fact, most current web-enabled applications are based on a four-tier architecture because presentation services are divided between the web server and the browser (see Figure 5-3). As a result, the term "n-tier client-server architecture" is often used to encompass the broadest range of applications.

Presentation Tier

The presentation tier is responsible for providing a mechanism for a user to interact with a client-server application (Figure 5-4). It is sometimes referred to as a *front-end*, a *user interface*, or a *client*. The standard way for a user to interact with an application is by providing input (e.g., filling in a data entry form) and receiving output (e.g., viewing a screen or printing a report).

What distinguishes various presentation tiers from one application to the next is the level of processing activity that occurs after receiving inputs and before providing outputs. If the presentation tier performs a great deal of processing activity, it is referred to as a *fat client* or a *rich client*. If the amount of activity performed at this layer is minimal, it is referred to as a *thin client* or a *lean client*.

In designing client-server applications, a great deal of consideration is usually given to splitting up the processing load among the various tiers. A thin-client architecture is most appropriate where the diversity of types of computers and operating systems being run by end users is high. This is because such a situation calls for maintaining multiple versions of the presentation software. Thin clients are also appropriate where users are highly dispersed geographically, including situations involving mobile users. Examples of thin-client applications are Internet-based retail outlets and programs that use bar-code readers to update inventories.

Conversely, a fat-client architecture is more appropriate in settings where the end-user platform is relatively uniform and the users themselves

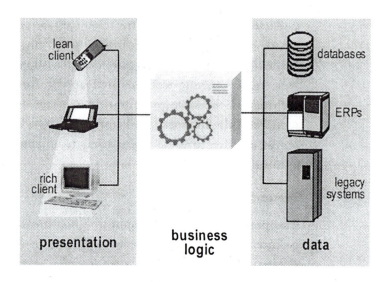

FIGURE 5-4. Three-tier client-server architecture.

work in a localized setting. Examples of fat client applications are word processing, spreadsheets, and desktop databases.

Business Logic Tier

The business logic tier is responsible for performing most of the processing that occurs in a client-server application (Figure 5-4). Exceptions to this include processing that is specifically related to obtaining inputs and presenting outputs to the user (presentation tier) and processing that is associated with storing and retrieving data from a database (data tier). One way to think of the business logic tier is that it comprises all of the behind-the-scenes computation or calculation that is defined by business-specific rules rather than more general rules that apply to the management of data. For example, the calculation of a customer discount involves the application of rules that are specific to the business and have nothing to do with how this information is stored or retrieved from a database.

The emergence of the business logic tier as a platform that is distinct from tiers providing user-oriented services and database-oriented services has revolutionized the development and deployment of information systems.

This middle tier has given rise to component-based computing where applications are composed of services provided by components that are distributed across networks in ways that are transparent to the end user.

Currently, applications based on distributed component computing are dominated by two competing architectures. Microsoft's strategy for the Windows platform is called Distributed interNet Applications architecture (DNA), and its component specification is called the Component Object Model (COM or COM+). Within this powerful framework, developers can build components in any language (as long as they abide by the COM specification) and deliver them on a wide range of platforms (but with a clear bias toward Windows operating systems).

Competing with Microsoft's DNA is Common Object Request Broker Architecture (CORBA) which has been developed and is maintained by the Object Management Group or OMG (a consortium of about 800 companies). CORBA components can also be developed in any language, but since the OMG's most vocal member is Sun Microsystems, the predominant language is Java.

Data Tier

As you can imagine, the data tier is responsible for data management, including the storage and retrieval of data from a range of possible sources (Figure 5-4). Commonly referred to as the *backend*, the data tier also provides backup and recovery services and transaction management.

The data tier is usually implemented on a minimum number of physical servers—ideally, just one (not counting fault-tolerant duplexed or mirrored servers). Splitting data across multiple servers is a highly complex and error-prone operation. The one major exception to this is when data are not highly integrated, as in the case of legacy information systems that are functionally oriented and narrow in scope.

Enterprise Architecture

Distributed systems in a large enterprise can be a nightmare to manage. In addition to the general loss of managerial control, there are numerous hidden costs associated with a client-server architecture. Studies have shown that distributed information systems require greater investments in operations and support, network administration, and training than totally centralized systems.

One solution to the managerial challenges posed by distributed systems is to define an enterprise information architecture. Rather than focusing on specific technology or equipment (that's infrastructure), an information architecture is a detailed definition of the goals, standards, and policies for the acquisition, deployment, and use of information systems across the enterprise.

Summary

This chapter began with a discussion of the evolution of corporate networks from the early days of LANs and WANs to their modern counterparts: the Internet, intranets, and extranets. Then, we introduced the managerial issues of distribution and control along with some of the challenges raised by distributed information systems. In the following section, we showed how connectivity can be addressed through transparent solutions, availability through reliable solutions, and performance through scalable solutions. The chapter concluded with a discussion of the three-tier client-server and the importance of developing enterprise information architecture.

Discussion Questions

1. What was it about the emergence of corporate networks that united both end users and IS managers? Which constituency do you think benefited most from networking? How has the Internet changed this balance of power?

2. Why is there such a tension between distribution and control of IT resources in today's corporations? Explain, using examples from your work or school environment.

3. Imagine yourself as the manager of a large corporate computer network. Faced with relatively equal demands by end users for connectivity, availability, and performance, which management strategy would be your foremost priority? Explain why.

4. Of the various technical approaches to providing connectivity, availability, and performance of distributed IT resources, which do you think is the most cost-effective approach? Explain why.

5. What are some advantages that are achieved by moving from a two-tier to a three-tier client-server architecture? from a three-tier to a four-tier architecture? Can you think of some disadvantages of increasing the number of layers in a network architecture? Why has the term "n-tier" become the most prevalent term for describing client-server networks?

References

Beyda, William J. *Data Communications: From Basics to Broadband.* Upper Saddle River, N.J.: Prentice Hall, 2000.

Duchessi, Peter, and InduShoha Chengalur-Smith. "Client/Server Benefits, Problems, Best Practices." *Communications of the ACM* 41, no. 5 (May 1998).

Huff, Sid, Malcolm C. Munro, and Barbara H. Martin. "Growth Stages of End User Computing." *Communications of the ACM* 31, no. 5 (May 1988).

Keen, Peter, and J. Michael Cummins. *Networks in Action: Business Choices and Telecommunications Decisions.* Belmont, CA: Wadsworth, 1994.

Moniz, Joseph. Enterprise Application Architecture. Birmingham, England: Wrox, 1999.

Chapter 6

Data at the Core of the Enterprise

There are no facts, only interpretations. — Friedrich Nietzsche

An enterprise system represents, in software, the business processes and state of an enterprise. The programs define and implement the processes, but processes without data are empty shells. Certainly, understanding the processes that an enterprise uses in order to fulfill an order is important. Data, however, describe the state of all of the enterprise's orders. Moreover, each order has a different state, defined by the data applicable to that order.

Obviously, describing all of the ongoing processes in even a small enterprise requires a great deal of data. The enterprise system must be capable of manipulating immense quantities of data in an efficient and timely manner. Of all the technologies that needed to reach maturity in order to enable enterprise systems, data management technology is arguably the most important.

We do not have sufficient space in this text to provide comprehensive coverage of the topic of Database Management Systems (DBMS). However, exposure to the main DBMS characteristics and capabilities is a necessary prerequisite to understanding enterprise systems. This chapter provides some background on DBMS in general, as well as a discussion of the evolution of the database from early application-based file systems through early DBMS models, and an overview of future directions in data storage and management. The basics of how the data is conceptually modeled and arranged or normalized for storage are introduced, as well as the way data is stored in and retrieved from the database.

Enterprise systems create new challenges for the database administrator (DBA). As we shall see, the size of an enterprise system database is overwhelming, being orders of magnitude larger than has been seen before. The sheer volume of data requires that database administrators develop new administration techniques to control the database. The DBMS is also the most important performance factor in the responsiveness of an enterprise system. As a result, both administrators and the enterprise system designers need to overcome some of the inefficiencies in standard DBMS to provide adequate response to the enterprise system users.

Data, Information, Knowledge

Recently, there have been many discussions in academic and business circles about the differences between data, information, knowledge, and wisdom. As people discuss these matters, the tendency is to add "management" to the end of the word so that we have data management, information management, and most recently knowledge management. Although these words possess some similarities, they in fact refer to different aspects of important corporate resources.

Data generally refers to facts that can be stored in a computer system that can be used to create information. Data have no inherent use or action of their own but requires some processing such as sorting, selecting, formatting, and the like, in order to create information. Databases were originally designed to be central repositories of data. The data repositories store the data one time in one place so that they (the data) can be extracted

VIDEO STORE SYSTEM EXAMPLE

Throughout this chapter, we will look at the evolution of a video store system that keeps track of video rentals by customer as well as an inventory of the films available. The film inventory will allow the store to discover who starred in what motion picture. The initial system begins with two files, one to keep track of customer and rentals, another to keep track of films and stars.

This is not a recommended, or even a particularly realistic, file setup for running a video store (don't try this at home). It is simply for illustrative purposes in this chapter. It is also not nearly as comprehensive as an enterprise database system would be. This system covers very few functions (part of inventory, accounts receivable, and customer relations), whereas an enterprise system would cover all of these areas in much more detail, and would integrate with other areas, too.

FILM ID	FILM NAME	STAR	NUMBER
5	Philadelphia Story	Jimmy Stewart Cary Grant Katherine Hepburn	12
7	Gone with the Wind	Clark Gable Butterfly McQueen Vivien Leigh	8
15	North by Northwest	Clark Gable Eva Marie Saint Alfred Hitchcock	6
43	Bedtime for Bonzo	Ronald Reagan	1
65	Pokemon XXVIII	Pikachu Raichu PsyDucck	28
97	Harvey	Jimmy Stewart	3
1432	Flying Tigers	Ronald Reagan	2

TABLE 6-1. Films and stars.

CUST ID	CUST NAME	STREET	CITY	OUT	IN	ST	ZIP	FILM NAME
7	Sophie Sanddune	123 A Street	Chico	1/1/99	1/20/99	CA	95929	Gone with the Wind
7	Sophie Sanddune	123 A Street	Chico	8/7/00	8/15/00	CA	95929	Flying Tigers
7	Sophie Sanddune	123 A Street	Chico	7/15/00	7/23/00	CA	95929	Bedtime for Bonzo
12	August Concrete	711 Haight	Chico	8/1/00	8/14/00	CA	95929	North by Northwest

TABLE 6-2. Customers and rental transactions.

and processed or used to meet the needs of many unique users. Examples of data include employee name, addresses, customer accounts, and vendor products. When someone in the company needs office supplies, he or she can call up the vendor product data and sort it by product name, extracting whatever specific pieces of data are needed. What the user gets then is information. It has value and has been transformed from the raw data state. If resulting information is then stored in the database, it becomes one component of knowledge.

Knowledge, therefore, has many contexts and is not a simple term to define. Academics have long been arguing over its definition. Similar to the differences in data, information, knowledge, and wisdom, knowledge in general is thought to have, at a minimum, information ("know what"), and "know how." Information is processed data that can be transferred from one person to another without loss of integrity. Know how, on the other hand, is the "accumulated practical skill or expertise that allows one to do something smoothly and efficiently" (vonHippel, 1988). If this is the minimum that knowledge entails, then the full dimension of knowledge includes the information (know what) and know how components, as well as the understanding (know why) and creative (care why) dimensions (Kogut and Zander, 1992).

Knowledge may have several dimensions that represent depth and scope for a particular topic. For example, with respect to job skills, one person may need to have only a basic skill, while others may be expected to understand the underlying assumptions of how and why something works the way it does. Others may be expected to take existing knowledge and create something new from it, adding still another use component to the knowledge definition. Therefore, knowledge contains information that is usually comprised of transformed data along with a use component that takes the information and adds either know how, know why, or care why dimensions. Knowledge management and knowledge warehouses represent the future trend in current data and information warehouse models.

Evolution of Data Architectures

Business data has been central to business computing since the beginning of the commercial use of computers, the early days of data processing. The idea that systems should be integrated, that the programs controlling

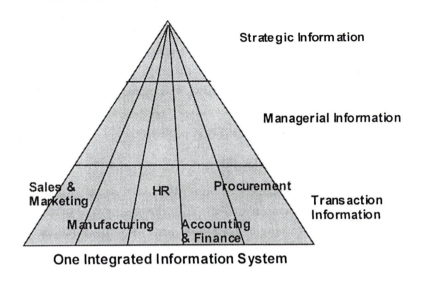

Strategic Information

Managerial Information

Sales & Marketing

HR

Procurement

Transaction Information

Manufacturing

Accounting & Finance

One Integrated Information System

FIGURE 6-1. Information requirements in Anthony's hierarchy.

different functional areas should operate on the same relevant information, has been proclaimed since the earliest days of wide-scale business data processing.

You will remember from Chapter 2 that Anthony (1965) viewed the business organization as a pyramidal structure. As one goes up the pyramid, the information provided by a management information system (MIS) is tailored to support different types of decision. At the bottom of the pyramid, transaction data is most important since the MIS will support operational employees. As we go up, data is synthesized and summarized in order to provide decision support information to middle management. At the highest levels of the organization, the information is summarized and used primarily to provide support for top management's strategic decisions (Figure 6-1). In order to be efficient and, more importantly, accurate, all of this information should come from a system that integrates the data from all operational area systems. Detail as well as summary information should be available to the manager as needed.

In 1965, neither the technology nor the state of the art in design could support such a model. With limited online storage capacity and limited memory, the computer systems of the 1960s and early 1970s simply did not have the resources or were too expensive to support the data requirements of enterprise systems.

Mainframe computer systems were the norm and only very large business entities could afford to buy them. Memory costs from the early 1970s for an IBM 360 mainframe computer were $.50 per byte of relatively slow main memory (Garside, 1980). That's more than half a million dollars for a megabyte of memory!

The Flat File

During this era, data structures were defined by the programs that manipulated the data. Programs were written for a single application within a single functional area. The data layout for each program was defined within the source code of that program. It was possible for multiple programs to utilize the same data, but if the data definitions were modified by one program, all of the associated programs would need to be modified and recompiled before the data was usable.

The most common data structure of this era was the flat file. A flat file is a single file with rows representing records and columns describing the attributes of the data (much like an ordinary spreadsheet). Since no relationships are maintained among data files using such a structure, serious problems can result due to data redundancy, inflexibility, and lack of ability to share data among applications.

The Hierarchical Model

During the 1970s, 1980s, and 1990s, computer technology and capacity expanded dramatically. Storage of data and processing speeds, as well as the design methodologies to support such large-scale systems as enterprise systems, were now readily available. One consequence of these changes was the separation of data from process, known as program-data independence.

The first database model to implement program-data independence was the hierarchical model. This model was built on two major structuring concepts: Records and Parent Child Relationships (PCR). Records are accumulations of data fields, describing an entity in a business relationship. A parent record type could own multiple child records, thus creating a

PCR. A child record can be the parent of its own children's records in another PCR, but each record type was child to at most one parent. Any record type can only participate as a child in one PCR but is capable of acting as parent in several PCRs.

This model was capable of storing and managing vast quantities of data, and manipulating that data into valid and valuable operational information. This achieved one of the goals of database management–the management of realistic volumes of data to provide business value.

The hierarchical model, however, views all data relationships as strictly hierarchical. As such, the model is not expressive enough to support most business problems, particularly when the model must span functional boundaries and deal with the convoluted relationships between business information items.

The Network Model

Whereas the hierarchical model was created in the marketplace and defined by products that supported the model (primarily IBM's IMS), the network model emerged as the result of a governmental and industry effort to provide a standard for data management systems. Among the goals of the Data Base Task Group of the Conference on Data Systems Languages (CODASYL), the standards-setting body, was to overcome the inflexibility of the hierarchical model by providing a model that could support more complex business relationships among types of data.

The main structuring concepts in the network database are the Record or Record Type and the Set. As in the hierarchical model, a Record is a named set of related data fields. A Record Type consists of all the Records with the same definition. A Set is a one-to-many relationship between an owner Record Type (the Set Owner) and many member Record Types (Set Members). The Set of a single Set Owner and all the Set Members for that Owner are referred to as a Set Instance or Set Occurrence. A Set Member may only be a member in one occurrence of a named Set, but the member may be a part of other Sets.

The modeling capabilities of the network data model were expressive enough to portray complex relationships between the data elements in a business. The model was robust enough to handle as much data as could be stored at the time. Performance was adequate to answer complex queries and maintain large amounts of data very efficiently.

The major drawback to the network model was not its expressiveness, but its rigidity once design was complete. All set relationships needed to be specified during the design phase. Every query that the user might wish to ask had to be thought out prior to completion of design. If a new question was to be asked of the data, a set needed to be in place to supply the information. If no appropriate set existed, the data model had to be modified and affected programs also had to be modified. Modification of the model was not trivial work, and severe backlogs existed in IS departments in order to service change requests.

So, whereas the hierarchical model was not expressive enough to satisfy widespread data management needs, the network model was not flexible enough to cope with the constantly changing business scenarios. Furthermore, there was no theoretical basis for how the database should work.

The Relational Model

In 1970, E. F. Codd published a paper describing a database management system whose data management rationale was based on mathematical set theory. This model would overcome both the modeling rigidities and the information retrieval difficulties of the earlier models. It would allow very expressive data models, as well as permit users to use a standardized language to implement ad hoc queries against the database.

This expressiveness and flexibility did not come without a cost. The theoretical requirements of the model tended to make its implementation very inefficient. This conceptual model pushed the technical state of the art in 1970 to such an extent that it was more than 10 years before the available technology could adequately support the model. The first commercial implementation of relational database management systems (RDBMS) was made available in the early 1980s.

The major structuring tenets of the relational model are attributes, tuples, relations, and relationships between tables. Attributes, less formally called columns, are essentially data fields, with the added restriction that they must be atomic. Related attributes are collected together in tuples, known as rows less formally and as records in traditional data processing.

Groups of related tuples are held in relations or, less formally, tables or entities. Tables are essentially files in traditional data processing. If properly constructed, a relational model will store a single piece of information only once in the database. Other tables that need access to that piece of information will be able to use relationships to retrieve that data.

Every tuple in a relational database must have an attribute or combination of attributes that uniquely identifies it. This is known as a **key**. Any combination of attributes that map to only one occurrence of data in a database can act as a key. An example of this is the CUST ID field in the Customer File in our example. By knowing the CUST ID, we can retrieve the name of the customer, as well as the customer's address.

By including the key of one table as a **foreign key** in another table, we can establish relationships between the tables. An example of this would be including the CUST ID in a tuple that deals with rentals and keeping customer address information in a Customer file. This would allow us to retrieve customer information when we need it. We can follow this string of relationships to find whatever related information we need in the database.

This model is very flexible and allows the designer to model rather complex relationships within the data. The model does not, however, reflect the behaviors of the entities that are modeled. Furthermore, the model suffers from potentially serious inefficiencies. Since the model is designed to support ad hoc queries, there is no explicit provision for predesigned search paths and pre-tuned queries. As such, an unplanned query might end up performing string comparisons across gigabytes of data; this is a very slow process even on the fastest computers.

The Object Model

The relational model was adequate for complex data modeling and large-scale data management for several years. As time and technology moved on, however, some felt that the model was lacking in expressiveness and ease of use. Modifications to one relation in the data model often affected many other relations, and the designer would have to find all of the affected relations in order to ensure that changes were not destructive. With greater technical and design capabilities, many felt that the business objects managed within a database should go beyond just a data representation and that it should be possible to store actual business objects that contained both data and behavior. Also, as data storage requirements moved from the megabyte to gigabyte to terabyte range, the inefficiencies of the relational model were becoming intolerable.

The object design and development methodologies of the late 1980s and since were largely motivated as an attempt to handle programming in the large. Enterprise systems are a perfect example of programming in the large, although current major enterprise systems typically run atop a relational database management system. There is a great deal of sentiment and contention about moving from RDBMS to an object model. Many feel that the relational model is entirely adequate. Many others feel that the relational model's shortcomings make it inadequate now and are bound to make it more inadequate as users wish to model more and more complex processes.

The object model for database management has many advantages. It clearly offers a very enriched method of developing data and process models. By combining state and behavior in a single encapsulated object, very complex interactions and business situations can be effectively modeled. This gets past many of the conceptual limitations of the relational model. The model is extensible and scalable, since with encapsulation and data/ method hiding significant changes can be localized to a single object, and changes can be trusted not to cause serious side effects in other portions of the system. With the increasing complexity of enterprisewide processes and business objects that need to be represented and maintained in the database, the move to an object basis is inevitable. The data retrieval model in an object database management system is also far more efficient, though somewhat less flexible, than in the relational model.

Adopting the object database model presents some serious drawbacks, however. Both technology and methodology must mature in order to take full advantage of the model. There is a lack of agreement on a standard object-oriented data model, and there is no universally accepted model of what such a standard should be. This makes adoption of such a model upon which to base the information needs of an enterprise very high-risk. Such models are also currently on the bleeding edge of technology. Without much experience or much of a roadmap in developing very large-scale object systems based on an object-oriented database management system, such development is a pioneering effort.

The move to an object database model is inevitable because the advantages of the model are so great. The roadblocks, though, are serious. It can be taken for granted that the technical and methodological issues will be solved. Yet the definitional and standard issues are much more complex, and they must be resolved before there is any chance for wide-scale adoption of the object database management model.

Database as the Foundation for Enterprise Systems

A database management system is arguably the single most necessary component in creating an enterprise system. The DBMS must support a data model that is expressive enough to represent all of the transactions that a business enterprise must participate in. The model must be flexible enough to span the boundaries of functional areas and to be able to correctly reflect the consequences of a transaction in one functional area within a totally distinct functional area.

If the technology was not economically prohibitive, even the flat file model of the 1950s would be capable of supporting the volume of data required to support an enterprise system. But supporting the data volume alone is not sufficient. The data must also be managed as a whole, flexible enough to be shared and changed without a major overhaul of the system, and capable of expressing complex relationships and interconnections. This is the role of the database management system, and without this support enterprise systems could not exist.

Database Fundamentals

In addition to the immense changes that occurred in the available technology to support the volume of data required of an enterprise system, methods of conceptually dealing with the data have evolved. Changes have occurred in the way data are viewed and arranged in systems that has provided the flexibility necessary to model business objects. Two changes stand out as moving the ability to model data into the realm of feasibility: normalization and Entity Relationship Diagrams (ERDs). The development of a nonprocedural standard language (SQL) to support the relational model also moved the field ahead in terms of manageability of large volumes of data.

Data Modeling

In order to control and manage large volumes of data, developers need to be able to conceptualize it. They must be able to visualize both the data attributes that need to be controlled and the relationships between those attributes. And they need to know that their data will behave correctly and not cause any unintentional problems for the system. A process known as normalization can solve the latter problem. A particular type of diagram known as an Entity Relationship Diagram or, more familiarly, an ERD helps solve the former problem.

Normalization

Anomalies: In order to manage large amounts of data, the data must be well behaved. By well behaved, we mean that each item of data is stored only once (no data redundancy) and dissimilar data is not stored together as a unit. If either of these requirements is violated, anomalies are possible.

The three major types of anomaly are: insertion, modification and deletion. An insertion anomaly occurs when information about two dissimilar data types is stored together as a single data element. For instance, when customer name is stored with customer rental, we cannot insert a rental into our database without a customer being associated. This is probably reasonable. Conversely, however, we cannot add a customer into our database unless we have an associated order. This is very likely a problem, because we would probably like to add customers before they rent from us. The problem with this situation is that, although customers and rentals are associated, they are not the same things. This should be represented as two business objects, a customer and a rental. This is known as an insertion anomaly since it prevents us from rationally inserting data into our database.

A modification anomaly occurs when we store the same piece of information multiple times within our database. When and if the information changes, the update must be carried out wherever the data is stored. Again, if we stored customer information with each rental and a customer moved, the customer's address would need to be modified. If the customer's address was stored with each customer rental, then the address would have to be changed on each order to keep our database consistent.

This is known as a modification anomaly because it prevents modification of information from being carried out in a rational manner.

Finally, a deletion anomaly occurs when we inadvertently delete information that we need to maintain as a side effect of deleting other information. Assume that our policy is to purge rentals from the system after six months in order to maintain a reasonable amount of data. If we stored our customer information only with the rentals and a customer had not rented a film in six months, we would lose all of our information about that customer when we deleted the last rental record for that customer. Obviously, we do not want to lose our customer information when we delete rental information. This is a deletion anomaly where we lost valuable information because the data were not stored rationally.

The problem with this data is obvious, and we can prevent anomalies by following two simple rules: (1) Store data only one time within the database; and (2) never store semantically different data together. These rules are fairly obvious and in the simple scenario presented here would be easy to apply. In a real business situation, with many attributes, many business entities, and many relationships, however, the rules would not be as easy to apply. We have a series of steps, the normal forms, which we can follow to help us achieve these goals.

Keys: The concept that ties a relational database together is the idea of the key. A key is a single attribute from a relation or a collection of attributes that will uniquely identify a row in a relation. For instance, if we know the ID of a customer (generally assigned by the system), we can find information about that customer by looking up the ID. That ID is unique to a single customer. If we know a customer's name, however, that may or may not be unique. We can't be certain that knowing a customer is named Sophie Sanddune will allow us to look up information about the correct Sophie Sanddune. More than one customer might have that name.

This relationship is based on business rules that regulate the data. It is a business rule that a customer ID maps to one customer. There is no rule in our business, however, stating that customers need to have unique names. Although it might seem that the key relationship is an inherent quality of the data itself, it is really a reflection of the rules that regulate the data.

Keys allow the database to implement relationships between tables without repeating the data that's stored in the database. If Sophie Sanddune

NORMALIZATION OF THE VIDEO STORE SYSTEM: FIRST NORMAL FORM

For a table to conform to the relational model, each intersection of a row (record) and column (attribute) must have only one value. This is referred to as First Normal Form (FNF). Whenever we have Multi-Valued Attributes (MVAs) in a table, we must move these repeating attributes to their own table and connect the new table to the original table by including the key value from the original table.

FILM ID	FILM NAME	ACTOR ID	NUMBER
5	Philadelphia Story	7	12
		12	
		22	
7	Gone with the Wind	95	8
		34	
		66	

TABLE 6-1A. Film table.

Our Film file has an MVA. Because a film can have many actors, the Actor attribute can occur from one to many times in each record (see Table 6-1, page 89). To put the table in FNF, we need to remove the repeating values (Actors) and place them in their own table with a key value. The result is shown in Tables 6-1A and 6-1B.

ACTOR ID	ACTOR NAME
7	Jimmy Stewart
12	Cary Grant
22	Katherine Hepburn
95	Clark Gable
34	Butterfly McQueen

TABLE 6-1B. Actor table.

FILM ID	FILM NAME	NUMBER
5	Philadelphia Story	12
7	Gone with the Wind	8

TABLE 6-1C. Revised film table.

We can see that the Film table still has an MVA. Actor IDs can still occur multiple times in a record. Therefore, we must apply the FNF correction one more time. This time, however, we will modify the Film table (Table 6-1C) and create a third table that connects the two entities (Table 6-1D).

We've taken one table that had MVAs in it and made it into three tables that have no MVAs and are thus in FNF. By tracing keys from the Actor to Film table, we can see who starred in what films, and we can also see what films an actor starred in. We have also put both tables into First Normal Form.

FILM ID	ACTOR ID
5	7
5	12
5	22
7	95
7	34
7	66

TABLE 6-1D. Film-Actor table.

NORMALIZATION OF THE VIDEO STORE SYSTEM: SECOND NORMAL FORM

Only after a table is in first normal form can we then put it into second normal form (2NF). To put a table in 2NF, we inspect each row in a table to ensure that there are no Partial Key Dependencies. Partial Key Dependencies can occur only when we have a composite key in a table. (A composite key is a key that is made up of more than one attribute.) If any of the attributes in a table, which can be identified by the whole key, can also be identified by a subset of the attributes that make up the key, we have what is called a partial key dependency. This is a 2NF violation.

To alleviate 2NF violations, we once again make a new table. We move the attributes that are partially dependent to their own table, and we store them with the part of the key on which they depend. We still have the partial key in the main table that points to the new table, so we have not lost any information. We can retrieve the removed information by querying the new table with the part of the key.

CUSTOMER ID	CUSTOMER NAME	STREET	CITY	ST	ZIP
7	Sophie Sanddune	123 A Street	Chico	CA	95929
12	August Concrete	711 Haight	Chico	CA	95929

TABLE 6-2A. Customer table.

So, a table is in 2NF if it is in first normal form (no MVAs) and if no partial key dependencies exist in the table. Everything in the table depends on the whole key.

Our Customer and Rental table exhibits 2NF problems (see Table 6-2, page 89). The problem here is that we have stored customer information with rental information. The key that would identify each record in this table is a combination of CUST ID and FILM NAME. However, if we know CUST ID, we also know CUST NAME, STREET, CITY, ST, and ZIP. That is because these data fields rely on only part of the key (CUST ID), and not the whole key (CUST ID, FILM NAME). In order to solve this problem, we need to create two tables: one to hold customer information, and one to hold information about the rental (Table 6-2A, Table 6-2B).

CUST ID	FILM NAME	OUT	IN
7	Gone with the Wind	1/1/99	1/20/99
12	Harvey	7/15/98	7/22/98
7	Flying Tigers	8/7/00	8/15/00

TABLE 6-2B. Rental table.

The insertion, modification, and deletion anomalies that were present in the initial table are now alleviated. We can add customers without needing them to rent a film. We can delete rental transactions with no fear of deleting crucial customer information. We might want to take advantage of our Film file at this point and integrate that with the rentals by including the FILM_ID rather than the FILM NAME field in the rental table (Table 6-2C). This is a more satisfactory situation, since we now only need to store the film title one time.

CUST ID	FILM ID	OUT	IN
7	7	1/1/99	1/20/99
12	97	7/15/98	7/22/98
7	1432	8/7/00	8/15/00

TABLE 6-2C. Revised rental table.

Normal Form	Requirements
First Normal Form (1NF)	Each cell (intersection of row and column) has only one value; all entries in same column (attribute) must be same type; no rows are identical
Second Normal Form (2NF)	Must be in 1NF; no partial dependencies (all nonkey attributes depend entirely on all of key)
Third Normal Form (3NF)	Must be in 2NF; no transitive dependencies
Boyce-Codd Normal Form (BCNF)	Must be in 3NF; every determinant is candidate key

TABLE 6-3. Requirements of normal forms.

rents a video, all we need to store with that rental information is her customer ID. By referring to that ID, we can see whom to bill, possibly which credit card to bill, where to ship the merchandise, and any other customer information that is required by the transaction.

Normalization: Normalization is the process of ensuring that redundant data is not stored in the database, that anomalies are not present in the data model being created, and that all relationships between data are preserved so that all relevant information can be retrieved from the database. Normalization is divided into different steps or forms, each of which is more stringent than the previous form.

Applying the rules of each Normal Form will allow us to systematically separate data into well-behaved tables and relations that will be free from anomalies and will ensure that the database is free from redundant data. It begins by making sure that each data element in the database is atomic (has only one value), and it continues to make sure that key relationships are proper and data is nonredundant.

The normalization example in this text is only pursued to Second Normal Form. Several more forms of normalization can be applied (see

Table 6-3). Every normal form, however, causes performance degradation in the database. There is always a tradeoff between the extra look-ups that normalization requires and the ease of modification and application development. It is common to normalize a database and then denormalize it in order to balance performance characteristics with ease of maintenance and cleanness of the data model. As long as the denormalization is well documented, the application can be developed in such a way that anomalies can be handled without a large performance penalty. It is common in very large systems, such as enterprise systems, to let the application code handle some of the normalization tasks.

Normalization is what is known as a *bottom-up* technique. We start with the specific detail, in this case a listing of all the attributes that the database must maintain, and we build a more general picture of the data model by iteratively refining the relations or tables that exist in the data. The end result of the normalization steps is a set of well-behaved tables. Each attribute in each table will be dependent only on the table's key. The key relationships between the tables will ensure that no information is lost when we decompose the tables. Finally, we can be reasonably assured that there is no redundant data in the database, and no anomalies will occur when we manipulate the data.

Entity Relationship Modeling

In contrast to normalization, Entity Relationship (ER) modeling is a *top-down* technique. In ER modeling, we develop a model that focuses on the entities (or tables) necessary in our database and on the relationships between the entities. By taking this approach, we achieve a semantic understanding of the problem domain, and we construct a data model that logically describes and fits the domain. This model, if properly constructed, can be expected to support any processes that are defined within the problem domain.

ER modeling is generally associated with the relational database management model, but it is not really confined to this environment. ER modeling may also be successfully utilized to describe, define, and create Network and Object data models. Regardless of the underlying model for which we are defining the ER model, the standard outcome of ER modeling is an Entity Relationship Diagram (ERD). A *conceptual ERD* will define

SIX STEPS TO CREATE AN ERD FOR THE VIDEO STORE SYSTEM

The steps of creating an ERD are reasonably simple. In the following, we describe six essential steps to create an ERD.

Step 1 Make a list of the entities to be modeled. An entity is anything that is to be represented in the data model. These are the items in the environment that we are interested in collecting and controlling data about. In the relational model, each of these entities will be converted to a table in the database.

In our example database, entities that we are interested in are **Customer, Film, Actor,** and **Rental** transaction.

Step 2 Describe the relationships between these **entities** in terms of cardinality and modality. Cardinality defines how many of one type of entity can be related to another entity. For instance, a customer can have many rentals, but a rental will only have one customer. This is a one-to-many relationship between Customer and Rental. The options for cardinality are one-to-one, one-to-many, and many-to-many.

Modality describes the participation of an entity in a relationship. For example, we can have a Customer with no rentals, so a Customer's participation in the Customer/ Rental relationship is partial. We cannot have a Rental, however, without an associated Customer. Thus, Rental participates fully in the Customer/Rental relationship.

The relationships in our database are as follows:

A customer can rent many films. A film (title) may be rented by many customers (many-to-many).

An actor may appear in many films. A film may have many actors (many-to-many).

Step 3 Decide which attributes are important or what information we want to store about each entity. This will create the list of attributes that need to be stored to fully specify the data model that we are creating.

In our database, we wish to store the following information:

Customer: Name, Street Address, City, State Zip
Film: Film Name, Number in Stock
Actor: Actor Name
Rental: Date Rented, Date Returned

Step 4 Designate the primary key columns. Decide what data we will use to uniquely identify each row or record in each entity that we have created. This is the first step in which we are starting to think of physical data storage. This also lets us identify what information needs to be stored, such as Customer ID, in order to identify the unique occurrences in our tables. Often, this data needs to be specifically generated in order to satisfy the requirements of the data model that we are using.

In our database, the following system generated fields will be used as primary key columns:

Customer: Customer ID (numeric field)
Film: Film ID (numeric field)
Actor: Actor ID (numeric field)
Rental: This is known as a dependent relationship or a weak entity. It cannot exist without its parents (Customer and Film) and can be identified by its parents. Thus, it has no primary key of its own but will have a key made up of its parents' keys.

At this point we have our conceptual ERD (Figure 6-2).

SIX STEPS TO CREATE AN ERD FOR
THE VIDEO STORE SYSTEM (CONTINUED)

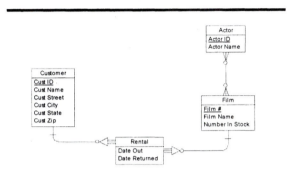

FIGURE 6-2. Conceptual ERD.

Step 5 Implement relationships among the entities. Here we are creating a physical model of the database and letting the DBMS know how to tie the relationships together. There are specific ways that this is achieved in the relational model.

(a.) A one-to-many relationship is implemented by placing the key of the entity on the one side into the many-side entity as a foreign key.

(b.) A one-to-one relationship is implemented by placing the key of one entity into the other entity as a foreign key. Generally, one entity will fully participate in the relationship, and one will partially participate. It is best to take the key of the entity that partially participates and to place that foreign key into the entity that fully participates.

(c.) A many-to-many relationship cannot be directly realized in a relational database system, since that would require a first normal form violation. To implement a many-to-many relationship, we need to create a new entity that connects the two entities. This entity will have a composite primary key consisting of the primary keys of the two entities that share the relationship. In this way, the multivalue attributes associated with the many-to-

many relationship will be stored as single-value attributes in the connecting entity.

This creates the physical database design, which is ready to be implemented as a relational database. This can be seen in Figure 6.3. The relationships were implemented as follows:

Actor to Film: Since it's many-to-many, a new relationship was formed, containing the primary keys of both the Actor table and the Film table.

Rental: Since this was a dependent entity, it can be seen that a new primary key was created formed of the combination of FILM_ID from the Film table and CUST_ID from the Customer table.

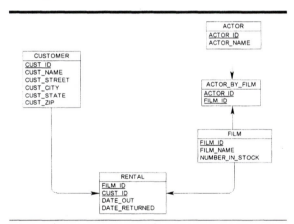

FIGURE 6-3. Physical ERD.

Step 6 Evaluate the design. We can evaluate the design in terms of how well the model represents the business entity that we have designed. We can also evaluate the design in terms of technical quality by applying the rules of normalization to the model in order to ensure that anomalies don't exist in the data.

the data model without any consideration of implementation details. The conceptual ERD will be transformed into a *physical ERD* that will provide the implementation detail that will support the physical constraints of the database model being constructed. (The steps to creating an ERD are described in the context of the video store system example on pages 104 and 105.)

ERDs are represented according to several different symbol sets. The symbol sets represent entities, relationships between the entities, and special symbols that indicate the cardinality and modality of the relationships. Generally speaking, a relation (which will be translated as a table) is represented by a rectangle. A relationship is represented as a line between the rectangles (tables). Cardinality and modality are represented by the symbolic way that the line is terminated.

For enterprise systems, ERDs are typically enormous and complex. The ERD supporting SAP R/3, v 4.0, for instance, consists of more than 15,000 tables and the relationships between them. Each business process that the enterprise software will support needs to be modeled, and it needs to be specialized enough that it can support the appropriate business requirements. Normalization is enormously important in such an environment since any anomaly can be extremely difficult to control. Thus, both top-down and bottom-up approaches to modeling the data must be employed in order to fully implement such a complex data model.

SQL

In 1986, the American National Standards Institute (ANSI) and the International Standards Organization (ISO) developed and standardized a nonprocedural language to support relational databases. This language was called the Structured Query Language or, more commonly, SQL. SQL allows relational database users to send either preplanned or ad hoc queries to the database and retrieve information.

The user does not need to know how to program, since the language is nonprocedural. SQL decides how it will implement the request for information, which is not necessarily a good thing. (It can be very inefficient and often must be tuned, as will be discussed under Data Administration.) Unlike earlier models, the question to be asked does not need to be preplanned. Thus, ad hoc queries of the database are possible. A user can ask for information from the database that the developer did not conceive of during development.

We can separate the basic SQL constructs into three major areas. One is DDL, or Data Definition Language. DDL allows us to create and alter database objects, such as tables and constraints on the tables. We can also drop or delete database objects. The other two areas are in DML, or Data Manipulation Language. One set of commands allows us to add, change, and delete data to the database. The other set allows us to retrieve data from the database, and combine the information in the database during retrieval.

Database Definition: The most important DDL commands are CREATE, ALTER, and DROP. CREATE allows us to create database objects such as tables. An example, which would create our Customer table, is as follows:

```
CREATE TABLE CUSTOMER
          (CUST_ID           NUMBER(5),
          CUST_NAME          CHARACTER(20),
          CUST_STREET        CHARACTER(20),
          CUST_CITY          CHARACTER(20),
          CUST_STATE         CHARACTER(2),
          CUST_ZIP           NUMBER(5));
```

The preceding SQL statement would create our Customer table and create the necessary columns to hold the data in the table. We do not have a primary key column in this table, but we could easily alter the table in order to create such a column, using the SQL ALTER command.

```
ALTER TABLE CUSTOMER
     ADD CONSTRAINT CUSTOMER_PK
          PRIMARY KEY (CUST_ID);
```

This ALTER command would change the structure of the CUSTOMER table by adding constraint (CUSTOMER_PK) that would set a primary key for the table, and it would make the CUST_ID attribute the primary key. It would also force the table to treat CUST_ID as a primary key field by adding NOT NULL and UNIQUE constraints to that attribute..

Finally, the DROP command allows us either to delete entire databases and tables, or, in conjunction with the ALTER command, delete parts of database objects. For instance, if we wanted to get rid of the primary key constraint from our Customer table, we could issue the following command:

```
ALTER TABLE CUSTOMER DROP CONSTRAINT CUSTOMER_PK;
```

And if we wished to get rid of the entire Customer table (along with all of its data), the following command would do that for us:

```
DROP TABLE CUSTOMER;
```

These commands do not take a great deal of technical expertise to use, and they allow us to easily create and modify our database structures. Furthermore, they run with little or no modification on any RDBMS that is SQL compliant.

Database Population: Once we have used DDL to create our database, we need to put data into the structure in order to process it. We will also, of course, have to remove data occasionally and modify the data that is in there. In order to achieve these respective ends, the commands INSERT, UPDATE, and DELETE are used.

INSERT will add data to the database as long as all constraints are met. We cannot have duplicate primary keys, we must have values for all of the mandatory fields, and we can't violate foreign key constraints. (We can't, for instance, add a record for a customer to the rental table if that customer ID is not available in the customer file.) Let's add August Concrete to the Customer file. We would do that as follows:

```
INSERT INTO CUSTOMER
        (CUST_ID, CUST_NAME, CUST_STREET, CUST_CITY, CUST_STATE,
        CUST_ZIP)
VALUES
        (12, 'August Concrete', '711 Haight', 'Chico', 'CA', 95929);
```

Notice that the INSERT statement includes both the data fields that the data will go into, and the data that is to be entered into the table. As long as 12 is a unique Customer ID, and as long as all data elements are of the right data type, this information will be successfully added to the database.

Modification of the data is handled via the UPDATE SQL statement. In order to update a record, however, we need to tell the database which record we wish to modify. We do this with a WHERE clause, that will isolate the record to be modified. In the case of our customer file, we can isolate the record we wish to modify by using an attribute we know will return a unique record: the CUST_ID. If we wish to change August Concrete's name to August Canola, we can do it with the following command:

```
UPDATE CUSTOMER SET CUST_NAME = 'August Canola'
     WHERE CUST_ID = 12;
```

This would change the CUST_NAME attribute of August's customer record from August Concrete to August Canola. Furthermore, since the database is normalized, wherever we refer to August we do it as Customer 12, and this single change will cause his name to be changed wherever it is referenced in the database.

Deletion of data from the database is accomplished via the DELETE SQL command. This command is dangerous, since if we issue the perfectly correct command

```
DELETE FROM CUSTOMER;
```

we will delete all of the information from the Customer table, whether or not we want to. We can solve this problem by judicious use of the WHERE clause with the delete in order to delete only the rows we want. If we wish to delete only August's record from the Customer file, knowing that his Customer ID is 12, we can issue the following command:

```
DELETE FROM CUSTOMER WHERE CUST_ID = 12;
```

This would only remove the desired record. If we wished to delete all film rentals returned prior to 1/1/99, we could issue the following command:

DELETE FROM RENTAL WHERE DATE_RETURNED < 1/1/99;

These commands will work with little alteration across all SQL-compliant relational databases. This allows a person trained on one database system, say Oracle, to transfer her knowledge and understanding to other platforms such as SQL Server or Informix, with a minimal amount of retraining.

Data Retrieval: The average end user does not enter data manipulation commands to the database. The probability of an incorrect DELETE command and its consequences are too great to encourage the user to do this. The requirements to correctly issue UPDATE or INSERT commands are rather onerous in practice. Thus, most data entry and modification are done through programs that issue the SQL statements to the database. The user is protected from the database realities, and the database is protected from the user. Retrieving data, however, is a safe and necessary activity that a user can conduct.

Data retrieval in SQL is performed using the SELECT command. This command allows the user to retrieve data from the tables in a nonprocedural manner. The user does not need to know how to access the tables or the order in which the access will take place. The user only needs to know the names of the attributes to retrieve and the names of the tables in which those attributes reside. Tables may also be JOINed, or combined, hopefully on key fields, in order to fill out information.

The general format of the SELECT command is:

SELECT attribute-names FROM table-names WHERE where-condition
    ORDER BY attribute name;

The WHERE and ORDER BY portions of the command are optional and do not need to be specified. If we wished to retrieve the name and street address of every person in the Customer table of the database, we would issue the following command:

```
SELECT CUST_NAME, CUST_STREET FROM CUSTOMER;
```

If we wanted them to be sorted by zip code, we could modify the command as follows:

```
SELECT CUST_NAME, CUST_STREET FROM CUSTOMER
    ORDER BY CUST_ZIP;
```

This is a single table select, which will allow the user to retrieve information from one of the entities in the database. The power of the SELECT statement, and, indeed, of the relational model, comes in joining the tables together in order to retrieve information. For instance, if we wanted to know all of the movies that were rented by all customers, we could issue the following command:

```
SELECT CUST_NAME, FILM_NAME
    FROM CUSTOMER, RENTAL, FILM
    WHERE RENTAL.CUST_ID = CUSTOMER.CUST_ID
    AND RENTAL.FILM_ID = FILM.FILM_ID
    ORDER BY CUST_NAME;
```

The WHERE condition here is known as a JOIN condition, since the records in the tables will be joined where that condition is true. The result of a SQL query is a temporary database table, and the user will be shown the results based on the contents of the temporary table. Furthermore, if we wished to see the results in film name order, we would only need to change the ORDER BY clause to have the results printed out by FILM_NAME rather than CUST_NAME.

If we wanted to find all of our movies that starred Jimmy Stewart, we would join the Film, Actor and Actor by Film tables. If we look at Figure 6.3, we can see that we have an ACTOR_NAME field in the ACTOR table, as well as an ACTOR_ID, which is the key. We have a FILM_NAME field in the FILM table, as well as a FILM_ID, which is the key. In ACTOR_BY_FILM, we have two foreign key fields, FILM_ID, which allows us to find the film name in the FILM table, and ACTOR_ID, which allows us to retrieve the actor's name from the ACTOR table. The SQL query to fulfill this request would be:

```
SELECT ACTOR_NAME, FILM_NAME
      FROM ACTOR, ACTOR_BY_FILM, FILM
      WHERE ACTOR.ACTOR_NAME = 'Jimmy Stewart'
      AND ACTOR_BY_FILM.ACTOR_ID = ACTOR.ACTOR_ID
      AND ACTOR_BY_FILM.FILM_ID = FILM.FILM_ID
      ORDER BY FILM_NAME;
```

This query will check the Actor table, looking for a record where the name is "Jimmy Stewart." It will find and retrieve that record, including the fact that the ACTOR_ID in that record is equal to 7. Now, all of the records in ACTOR_BY_FILM where the ACTOR_ID has a value of 7 will be retrieved, and each film record in the FILM table that has a FILM_ID equal to one of those records will be retrieved. Finally, the ACTOR_NAME and FILM_NAME attribute values will be displayed for the user.

As can be imagined, as a schema grows bigger, the complexity of the SQL joins will also increase greatly. SQL SELECT statements can become very complex, and there are very talented and capable programmers who specialize in creating efficient and effective SQL queries. The value of these commands, however, is the capability to simply ask questions of the data that have not been asked before, whether or not the database has been designed to support such queries.

A user with basic knowledge of the structure of the database can ask simple questions and retrieve valuable information without a great deal of computer training. A user with basic understanding of SQL can ask these same questions of many different databases without having to possess a great deal of product specific knowledge.

SQL and its capabilities are largely responsible for the success of the relational model. The capabilities of SQL allow the user access to data without requiring a great depth of technical knowledge, and they permit an amazing degree of flexibility in manipulating and retrieving data. The universality of the language across most relational database management systems provides great transfer of knowledge and an environment that a user can exploit without having to fully understand the enormous complexities of modern database management systems.

Data Administration

Access to data is crucial for a modern enterprise. In order to provide feedback to the enterprise, the data that defines the health or condition of the enterprise must be available in a timely and meaningful fashion. This data is often contained in an enterprise system that controls all of the functional areas of the enterprise. The enterprise system represents a potential single point of failure in an enterprise. If the enterprise system becomes unavailable, the enterprise cannot conduct its business. It is not only a single functional area that is down; rather, all functional areas of the enterprise are down.

With a global enterprise, 24/7 availability is crucial. Twenty-four hours a day, seven days a week, somebody somewhere on the planet may be relying on the resources controlled by the enterprise system. It may be customers who are trying to place an order from anywhere on the planet, production facilities in one continent, management facilities on another continent, or financial or production partners anywhere in the world. The business landscape is no longer a 9-to-5, one-location environment. It is crucial that the enterprise system be available for all users at all times.

Enterprise systems typically run on databases that are stretched to their limits. The data models supported are immense, the volume of data is overwhelming, and data volume tends to grow at an exponential rate. All of these issues stretch the scalability of the relational database management model and push current database software to its limits and beyond. This pushing of the limits has caused problems for database administrators in providing support for enterprise systems. DBAs have identified challenges primarily in the areas of providing availability to the data resource and in providing timely access to the data contained in their enterprise systems (Connolly and Corbitt, 2000).

Performance and Tuning

Performance in a database can be measured by how quickly and efficiently data can be stored, retrieved, and associated within the system. If bottlenecks occur in the DBMS, data manipulation can become so slow as to bring the enterprise system to a halt. One of the jobs of the database administrator is to make sure that the system continues to operate in an efficient manner. "Tuning" the database or making sure that database environmental parameters are set so as to allow optimal performance does this. The DBA has to keep several features in mind when dealing with a DBMS in an enterprise system environment.

Enterprise systems typically provide their own set of tools for a DBA to use in controlling and monitoring the database. This adds an extra level of abstraction between the DBA and the database, since most DBAs are used to dealing directly with their database. Many DBAs find this extra layer a problem, since they feel secure in their ability to diagnose the database in its native mode. The enterprise system management tools tend to filter the information provided to the DBA. Since the relationship between the enterprise system and the DBMS tends to be complex and somewhat ill defined, the DBAs find it difficult to predict and confirm bottlenecks and areas of inefficient operation within the DBMS.

Data stored in the enterprise system is often not optimized for responses to SQL queries. Because the enterprise system requirements often exceed the limits that the database provides (for instance, number of tables in the entire database), the enterprise system takes advantage of nonnormalized tables and structures outside of the normal operation of the DBMS. SQL is not an extremely efficient language at best, and poorly formed SQL queries can be extremely slow. Unfortunately, sometimes the data is stored in an enterprise system in a way that is not conducive to quick selection. SAP, for instance, tends to store all data within a single company by a company code attribute. So all data within the company is partially identified by that company code, and a poorly formed SQL query would first retrieve all data for that company before refining the search.

If the DBA or a developer knows the storage structure of the data, SQL queries can be optimized and arranged in such a way that retrieval is efficient. Appropriate indexes can be added to the tables in the database in order to facilitate retrieval. A naïve query submitted by a developer, however, can be catastrophic in terms of an enterprise system's responsiveness. The DBA must be ever vigilant in ensuring that queries are well formed and properly designed.

DBAs can maintain their databases, with or without an enterprise system, in such a manner that it responds quickly and correctly to processing demands. The size of the data model that an enterprise system supports, as well as the volume of data that the enterprise system requires and the complexity of the programs involved, makes performance tuning even more of a challenge for the DBA. The breadth of the business processes that the enterprise system supports makes the job of providing adequate performance even more urgent than if the scope of the system were narrower.

Availability

The other major area of concern for enterprise system DBAs is availability of the system. If the database management system becomes unavailable, the enterprise system is unavailable. If the enterprise system is unavailable, the enterprise's computing resources are unavailable and the business can come to a standstill.

Availability means that the enterprise system is online and available for supporting the enterprise. The enterprise system provides two major challenges to DBAs in keeping the system available: predicting growth of the data in order to prevent database crashes which is very difficult; and backing up the data without taking the system offline which is a continuing problem for DBAs.

The growth of data in an enterprise system can be phenomenal. The enterprise system captures and stores all of the information that the entity generates. The enterprise system might contain a data-based description of every transaction that takes place in an entity on a global basis. This growth can be hard to predict and can lead to full log files as well as disk volumes that can contain no more data. These situations can cause a DBMS to unexpectedly cease operation. Particularly in the early days of a business organization's enterprise system, before there is an available history of data growth, this unexpected growth of data storage requirements can cause the system to become unavailable.

Even more perplexing is the need to back up the data in the system without going offline. The system must be available on a continual basis. One DBA describes backing up the database while online as similar to changing the tires on a bus while it is being driven down the street. The problems with data backup are exacerbated by two factors: the complexity of the transactions in the enterprise system and the volume of data served by an enterprise system.

A transaction in an enterprise system can update literally hundreds of tables. A backup takes time to perform. Whereas we may have backed up one table at time A, tables B and C might not have been backed up yet. By the time tables B and C are backed up, transactions that affect all three tables may have occurred. In this scenario, the tables will be out of synch. The data in table A is stale in relation to tables B and C, and restoring the tables from backup will cause a loss of data or corruption in the database. When we go from three tables to hundreds involved in a transaction, keeping the tables in synch is impossible while the system is online.

Volume of data is also a problem. While a true 24/7 database is a rarity, most enterprise system databases approach this. Typically, there is a four-hour weekly time window in which the DBA and system administrators can perform hardware maintenance, software upgrades, and administrative tasks such as backup. This is not sufficient time, however, to perform a sizable backup, even for a database that is less than 100 gigabytes. Many enterprise system databases have exceeded a terabyte of data today, and the physical time to transfer this data to backup media is measured in days rather than hours.

Faster technology is a partial answer to this problem, but it is not sufficient to handle today's needs, much less the needs of tomorrow as these databases grow. Methods such as having a redundant system (duplicate hardware and software) whose sole purpose is receiving real-time updates and providing a backup of the data is a fairly common, though very expensive, solution to this problem. The redundant system solution is not without problems itself. If the primary system goes down, the backup system must operate as the primary, and when the primary system is back online, the roles must be reversed and the data must be synchronized again. Database backup is an area of ongoing research, and new solutions are being suggested and tested in order to put this problem to rest.

Without the database management system, the enterprise system will not be available. Thus, tuning the database is a crucial aspect of enterprise system administration. If the database cannot provide results in a timely manner, the enterprise system is useless. Making sure that the database is functioning at peak performance and that queries are running as efficiently as possible helps guarantee that the enterprise system will be responsive to the needs of the users and the enterprise. The data that the enterprise system contains defines the enterprise that it supports. Timely and efficient backups ensure that the data is available and secure. Since the enterprise system cannot be taken offline for long periods of time in order to perform regular backups, time spent on devising backup strategies and making sure that they do not negatively impact the enterprise system performance and availability is time well-spent. These are crucial areas in the usability and pertinence of enterprise systems.

Summary

This chapter began with a discussion of the relationship between data, information, and knowledge and their role as corporate resources. Next, the reader is provided with a background on database systems and their evolution from early file systems through object-oriented database systems. Following an explanation of the role of database management systems as a foundation for enterprise system, the fundamentals of how data are modeled and normalized, manipulated using structured query language, and managed using modern methods of data administration are introduced.

Discussion Questions

1. Assume there are no resource-scarcity issues, but we are still in the days of file-based information systems. Think of ways we could implement an ERP in this environment. What technical issues would we face? What conceptual design issues would cause us problems?

2. In our example database, we have made a decision about rentals that is not necessarily good for the business. The setup has become a business rule via our implementation of the Rental table, however. What is this business rule? Why is it not necessarily good for our enterprise? How can we resolve this issue within the database design?

3. Many different media are now stored in relational databases. We wish to store pictures of our employees, actual scanned images of documents, sound data, and many other types of data that present issues in retrieval. For instance, we might want to retrieve the employee names of all of our employees who have beards, using the employee pictures to determine who should be selected. How would this be a problem in a RDBMS? What sorts of issues are involved? How could the problem be addressed, both within the relational model and in nonrelational models? What other types of data might present similar difficulties?

4. Grocery stores today often store data about specific customers through use of membership card systems. Your grocery receipt contains data about you, about the items you've purchased, historical data about your purchases, and even more information. Take one of your grocery receipts and create a database normalized to third normal form based on the data items on the receipt.

5. The preceding question was a bottom-up approach to database design, working from the actual data items represented to an overall database representation. Take the same receipt, and, based on your understanding of the data presented on the receipt, use the ERD approach to create a top-down model of the database. Are they similar? If the two models differ, explain how and why they would differ, and what different business rules would be represented in your solutions.

References

Anthony, Robert N. *Planning and Control System: A Framework for Analysis.* Harvard University, Graduate School of Business Administration, Division of Research, 1965.

Connolly, James, and Corbitt, Gail. "DBAs: Top 10 Issues in Administering Oracle for SAP." *Proceedings of the International Oracle Users Group–America Conference,* 2000.

Garside, R. G. *The Architecture of Digital Computers.* Oxford Applied Mathematics and Computing Science Series. Oxford: Clarendon Press, 1980.

Head, Robert V. "Management Information Systems: A Critical Appraisal."
    Datamation (May 1967): 22–27.

Kogut, Bruce, and Udo Zander. "Knowledge of the Firm, Combinative Capabilities,
    and the Replication of Technology." *Organization Science* 3, no. 5 (August 1992):
    383–397.

VonHippel, Eric. *The Sources of Innovation*. Cambridge, Mass.: MIT Press, 1988.

Chapter 7

The Architecture of an Enterprise System

We shape our buildings; thereafter they shape us. — Winston Churchill

Three key issues drive the development of enterprise systems architectures. First, enterprise systems must be able to run on a diverse range of hardware and software platforms. Second, to handle this diversity, standard technologies should be used for database management and standard protocols for data communication. And third, we need real-time support for key business processes throughout the organization, regardless of differences in local business environment.

OBJECTIVES

♦ Provide background on the architectural development of enterprise systems

♦ Examine logical and physical architecture enterprise systems

♦ Describe change transport in an enterprise system

In this chapter, we begin by reviewing some of the historical developments in information systems that have shaped enterprise systems architectures. Next, we examine enterprise systems architecture from both a logical and physical perspective. Finally, we describe how changes to an enterprise system are transported from development through production in a way that ensures reliable operation of these critical systems.

The Pursuit of Integrated Systems

The concept of enterprise systems can be traced back to the mid-1970s when database technology allowed, at least in principle, all applications to be supported by a common, centrally controlled database. As early as 1979, Richard Nolan and others proposed a *stage model* in which most organizations would go through an integration phase led by database technology.

Despite these early predictions, integrating all corporate information systems around a common database proved elusive for most organizations. There were many reasons for failing to adopt integrated systems, including corporate inertia, shifts in the popularity of different database technologies, and the emergence of client-server architectures. Occasionally, applications would appear that claimed to integrate a cluster of business functions. But due to many of the technical and organizational challenges discussed in Chapter 3, achieving a unified system that would support transaction processing in all parts of the organization remained just beyond the reach of even the most determined enterprises and software vendors.

Although early transaction processing systems were batch oriented, advances in communication, database, and scanning technologies allowed organizations to move to *online systems*. These systems captured transaction data simultaneously or very close in time to when events relevant to business functions occurred. Transaction data were then immediately posted to a database. Unfortunately, these early online systems were still fragmented and required data relevant to other systems to be transported using intermediate batch files. Surprisingly, fragmented information systems persisted through the era of centralized computing, and even when applications ran on the same mainframe computer, data usually had to be transported manually from one application to another.

The major thrust of enterprise systems was to correct this situation. Vendors like SAP had considerable experience in developing and integrating applications for many large firms. They used their expertise to develop integrated systems that supported a wide range of transaction processing functions that are common to most organizations. A firm adopting an enterprise system no longer had to spend valuable resources in developing applications from the ground up. Rather, they could customize a vendor-provided system by mapping their organizational structure and their business processes to a set of standard enterprise system functions. Enterprise systems included enough flexibility to allow for different operating structures as well as local currencies and tax laws.

Initially, enterprise systems were geared toward a centralized, mainframe-based computing environment, but these systems really came into their own with the shift in corporate computing toward distributed systems and client-server architectures. (SAP called its earlier system R/2 for real-time 2-tier architecture, and the current system R/3 for real-time 3-tier architecture.)

Most enterprise systems use commonly available relational database management systems (e.g., Oracle, DB2, SQL Server) and are based on standard network protocols (e.g., TCP/IP). This unbundling allows enterprise systems to run in heterogeneous computing environments and coexist with the widest possible range of hardware and operating systems platforms.

In the following section, we describe the architecture of enterprise systems with special focus on SAP R/3. (A similar architecture holds for the other major enterprise systems.)

Enterprise System Architecture

To understand the architecture of enterprise systems, it is necessary to examine them on two dimensions: (1) their logical architecture that defines the components and functionalities supported by the systems, and (2) their physical architecture that defines how specific components are implemented on computer and communication systems. In the following sections, we describe both dimensions.

Logical Architecture

At the heart of an enterprise system is a database that is a central repository of data needed to support common business processes. The database is organized so that data are entered into the system only once, and these entries are made as close as possible to the time of their corresponding business events. The data are then made available for processing in a series of steps that may add or modify the data in an incremental way. These

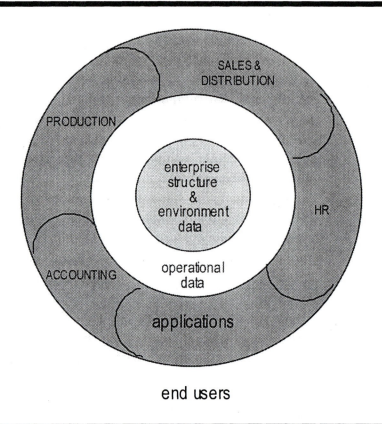

FIGURE 7-1. Logical architecture of an enterprise system.

data may also be made available to support the processing of transactions related to events other than original transaction. The transaction processing steps are organized so that all related steps are available together. Such grouping of routine transactional steps is defined as a "module." Thus, for example, the steps needed to complete an order fulfillment process might be aggregated as part of a sales and distribution module, the steps needed to generate financial reports could be grouped and located in an accounting module; and so on. This is schematically displayed in Figure 7-1.

At the center of the system is a common data repository that stores the operational data related to business transactions described above as well as data specific to the enterprise, including the enterprise structure and environmental data (e.g., tax tables, validation rules for addresses and telephones, currency conversion rates, etc.). In implementing an enterprise system, these enterprise-specific data are defined by setting the appropriate customizing switches, defining components of the enterprise and relating components to each other, and defining master data. The applications in an enterprise system remain the same for all customers. Of course, depending on the switches set in the customizing part, a customer may not use some application components.

In principle, all application components of an enterprise system are available to all users. Any limits to access are not inherent in the system (as would be the case if applications were not integrated) but are defined by the system administrator based on the specific activities performed by a user. In SAP R/3, for example, such limits are defined by associating a *profile* with a user.

Although Figure 7-1 shows the applications as being disjoint, the grouping of components is really around the underlying processes that may span functional and department boundaries. Thus, in the order fulfillment process, the transactions for generation of an invoice or for withdrawal of items from inventory would be automatically invoked. If the user has the right permissions (defined by the user profile in R/3), the resulting documents can be viewed and manipulated by the user. Moreover, operations on an application component are often found in more than one application module. For example, the master record for new material can be created in either the material management module or the production module.

One component is still missing from the conceptual model above. Since the operational database is constantly changing, people involved in analysis and planning-type activities often find it hard to use. To support these activities, an additional database layer called a *data warehouse* is built. The warehouse combines data from various internal and external sources and brings it together in a form so that it can be easily examined along many different dimensions and input into different analysis and planning models. Many enterprise system vendors including SAP and Oracle provide tools for building and populating a data warehouse.

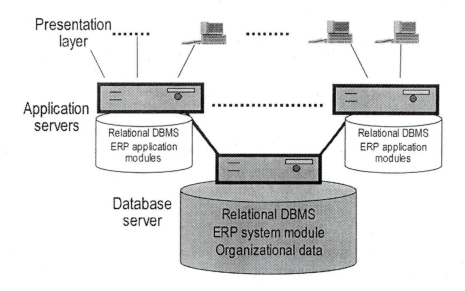

FIGURE 7-2. Three-tier architecture of enterprise systems. Objects that reside on application server include program modules (compiled), local buffers, and work processes. Objects that reside on database server include data dictionary, program modules (in source), organizational structure data, master and transaction data, log files, and global buffers.

Physical Architecture

To support the conceptual model above, a typical enterprise system utilizes a layered or tiered client-server architecture similar to what was discussed in Chapter 5. The layers that make up an enterprise system are the database layer, the application layer, and the presentation layer. The layered architecture of an enterprise system is depicted in Figure 7-2. Note that in the simplest case it is possible to implement all three layers on a single computer system. However, in a realistic environment each layer is implemented on a different computer or cluster of computers.

The Database Layer

The lowest layer in an enterprise system is the database that is implemented on a database server. The database engine is almost always a relational DBMS (e.g., Oracle, DB2, SQL Server) that can operate on many different hardware and operating system platforms.

In Figure 7-2, we have depicted the database server as a single machine. In practice, a database can be distributed across multiple servers. Distributed databases provide redundancy, robustness, and security and typically have locking features designed to avoid conflict among transactions being processed concurrently. To reduce both communications across networks and the frequency of disk accesses, database servers use intricate caching mechanisms whereby stored data is accessed only if the data in the cache is perceived to be stale.

The database for an enterprise system contains, in addition to the operational and enterprise structure data described above, items necessary for maintenance and recovery of the system, like data dictionary, transaction logs, archival files, and global buffers. In many enterprise systems, the source code of application programs is also stored as data within the database. For example, in SAP R/3 the source code for all application programs is stored in the database. The program components are compiled the first time they are needed. This is quite different from a traditional environment in which the operational systems work with only the object codes (compiled and linked programs in the machine language). Perhaps vendors like SAP chose to provide the source code to clients because it is easier to apply fixes to the system as errors are discovered.

The Application Layer

The middle layer of an enterprise system is the application layer that is made up of application servers. Typically, each application server is responsible for running a specific group of applications, although depending on the workload and other considerations, a unit of work may be routed to a different server. The application components at the application server are kept as compiled versions. In SAP R/3, for example, the first time a work unit requests a component, the source code is retrieved from the database

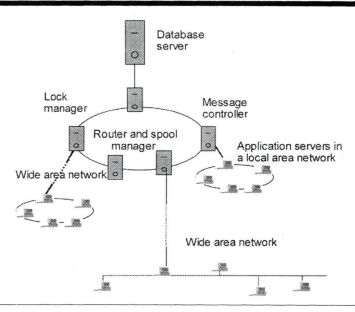

FIGURE 7-3. An implementation of three-tier architecture. Control functions like lock management, routing work units, and print spool management are also run at the application servers. Application servers in a local area network keep control messages localized and allow for dynamic load balancing.

and compiled. The compiled version is then kept at the application server and is available to all subsequent work units.

The application server also keeps application-specific data in one or more local caches. A local cache is synchronized with the data at the database server whenever some other application tries to access the same data. This reduces the necessity of frequent updates to the data at the database server, yet provides each application's most recent version of the data. If a component needs to be run at more than one server, a load balancing approach is followed in which work is routed to the least busy server.

The coordination between different application servers is achieved through the concept of a "work process." Each work process is associated with a unique task. Application components that allow users to work with the system interactively (for example, entering data for a sales order) bind to dialog work processes, whereas application components that generate background work (for example, generating a weekly sales report) bind to batch work processes.

Additional work processes coordinate activities between different servers and may only run on selected servers. These include a lock manager (that works with the database lock manager to allocate control of specific data items to an application component), a router (that routes incoming work to the appropriate server), a spool manager (that manages the printing of large files), and a message controller (that parses and routes messages to application servers and the database server, see Figure 7-3). In SAP R/3, an application server that contains all work processes is called a central instance and is responsible for all coordination activities. Since the coordination among different servers generates quite a bit of traffic over the network, it is customary to keep all application servers within a local area network that is typically located at the corporate data center.

The Presentation Layer

The presentation layer provides the interface between users and applications and is implemented as a set of menu-driven GUI screens. The presentation layer, or front end, may also be flexible enough to allow users to jump to a specific menu item rather than having to navigate through a complex menu system. For example, in SAP R/3 a user can jump to a screen by providing its "transaction code" (which is simply the identifier for the menu item). In fact, many experienced R/3 users prefer to use transaction codes to navigate through the system to working through the cumbersome menu system.

A presentation layer may be implemented locally on an individual user's desktop computer or on a presentation server within a local area network. The only purpose of the presentation layer is to accept essential data from the user and provide formatted reports to the user. Since the transaction data are actually processed at an application server, very little processing is done at the presentation layer. Therefore, these front-end clients do not have to be very powerful. In fact, SAP now supports its user interface on handheld machines with limited capabilities.

The presentation layer may keep, in a local storage, a list of recently invoked transactions and data specific to the process being supported. To control user access to programs and data items, and to limit the scope of

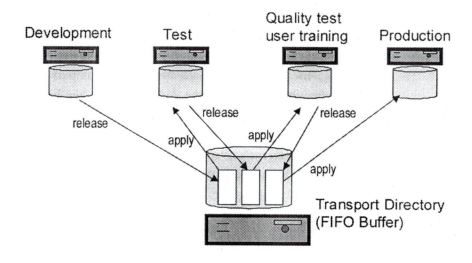

FIGURE 7-4. Propagating changes from development systems to the production system. Transport directory is kept at operating system level and is shared by all the systems.

transactions, the presentation layer is usually customized so that the user works with a limited menu. In addition, a customized presentation layer also allows for filling fields on input fields with default values or values retrieved from the database using a table look-up.

The presentation layer often includes additional graphic tools to support various development and reporting functions. For example, during customization, an organization's structure can be defined, and the customization projects and their components can be displayed graphically. Similarly during the operational phase, key operational parameters (e.g., system load, length of the print queue, number of active processes, etc.) may be displayed graphically with suitable color-coding to identify normal workloads, bottlenecks, and stopped work processes. To support analysis and planning activities, the presentation layer may also include packages to transfer data in reports to spreadsheets and other modeling and analysis tools.

Change Transport

Although the purpose of the three-layer architecture is to support enterprisewide activities using a common database, it makes the most sense for the operational or production system to be isolated from systems development and training activities. Like any other large system, enhancements and changes are typically done on a separate system and are incorporated in the production system only when the changes have been thoroughly tested, both for errors and its ability to perform under realistic workloads.

In enterprise systems, this issue becomes even more important since a small miscue may bring the entire operations of the enterprise to a standstill. In SAP R/3, this process is very carefully controlled. The overall process is called a *transport management system*. In this approach, each change is applied to the systems from development to production in a sequential manner. For each stage, the changes are applied in order so that all systems that have applied changes up to a particular change request match with each other.

The propagation of change from one system to another is coordinated through a *transport directory* that stores all change requests (at the operating system level rather than in a R/3 directory) and can be accessed by all systems. Each change has to be released by the previous system before it can be applied to the next system. Thus, we can think of transport directory as a series of *first in first out* (FIFO) buffers. When a system accepts a change, it is removed from the previous buffer and released to the next buffer. At the end of the chain, after the change has been tested for quality in realistic simulation of the actual workload, it is immediately applied to the production systems.

If, perhaps because of budgetary constraints, we have fewer IT resources, we may put two or more instances of R/3 on one physical computer system using a logical separation between them. Although this is acceptable for development, testing, and training systems, it is always preferred to maintain the production system on its own hardware.

In SAP R/3, logically separate systems that are implemented on the same hardware are called clients. While each client has unique customization data (e.g., company structure) and operational data (e.g., master and transaction data), they do share programs and certain data that are needed by all clients (e.g., application programs and data dictionary). One can imagine that if development and production systems were maintained on the same physical system, changes made by programmers would immediately affect the production environment before they had time to be adequately tested.

Summary

We began this chapter by reviewing some of the historical developments in information systems that have shaped the development of enterprise systems architectures. Next, we examined enterprise systems architecture from both a logical and physical perspective. Finally, we described how changes to an enterprise system are transported from development through production in a way that ensures reliable operation of these critical systems.

Discussion Questions

1. What situation became the major thrust for enterprise systems? Does this situation still exist in today's organizations? Do you think it is a common phenomenon? Explain why or why not.

2. What is the difference between a logical and a physical enterprise system architecture? Apply this difference by analogy to the architecture of a building or house, and describe both its logical and physical architecture.

3. How are changes transported in an enterprise system? What are some of the advantages of a multi-landscape architecture? What are some of its disadvantages?

References

Buck-Emden, Rudiger and Jurgen Galimow. *SAP R/3: A Client/Server Technology.* Harlow, England: Addison-Wesley, 1996.

Nolan, Richard L. "Managing the Crisis in Data Processing." *Harvard Business Review*, March/April 1979.

Saharia, Aditya N. and Kent Sandoe. "Enterprise Resource Planning (ERP) Systems." In Milan Zeleny (ed.), *The IEBM Handbook of Information Technology in Business*. London: Thompson Learning, 2000.

PART THREE

Building Enterprise Systems

E*nterprise systems implementation is the theme of the third part of this book. The complex, multi-phase implementation process is described over three chapters that cover initiating, planning, designing, realizing, and operating activities. This section concludes with a chapter on the roles that people play in both implementing and maintaining enterprise systems.*

Chapter 8

Planning for Enterprise Systems

In preparing for battle I have always found that plans are useless,
but planning is indispensable. – Dwight D. Eisenhower

Enterprise systems offer a range of opportunities to the organizations that deploy them. At their most basic level, enterprise systems allow organizations to integrate disparate systems and provide real-time information to employees, customers, and suppliers. In their fullest use, they enable firms to reengineer key business processes and ultimately restructure entire enterprises. But to take full advantage of these opportunities, organizations must be willing to undergo the massive, complex, often painful, and costly effort of enterprise system implementation.

This chapter begins by providing a context for understanding how information systems are built. The remainder of the chapter explains in detail the first phase of enterprise system implementation—project initiation.

OBJECTIVES

♦ Provide a high-level framework for enterprise systems implementation

♦ Explore the first phase of implementation: project initiation

♦ Describe the process of creating the project charter

Building Systems for Modern Enterprises

The way that information systems are made for and within organizations has changed considerably over the last 30 years. This section provides a context for understanding how enterprise systems are built in today's organizations. It begins with a description of traditional information systems development that has been dominated by programming within life cycle approaches. Next, a shift in emphasis away from development toward implementation is described. Finally, the six major phases of enterprise system implementation are briefly presented.

Traditional Development of Information Systems

Until fairly recently, the development of information systems has focused on the creation of software products or applications. In fact, the discipline of application development is often termed "software engineering," which is indicative of a highly technical and code-oriented process. This process is often described as cyclical, consisting of a series of steps or phases that ultimately return to the starting point as new software is created or old software is renewed.

The system (or software) development life cycle (SDLC) is a term that is used to describe this general approach, even though many variations on the SDLC exist in the academic and trade literatures (see Figure 8-1). The distinctive feature of most SDLCs is that all the activities they describe revolve around computer programs or code. Most of the early phases (feasibility, analysis, and design) focus on developing a clear description of the desired system for the programmers, while most of the later phases (implementation and operations) focus on testing, installing, and operating the resulting software.

Turning the Life Cycle Inside Out

During the past decade, there has been a shift away from the traditional life cycle approaches to system development. Instead of code-centric development of information systems, modern approaches tend to focus to a much greater degree on implementation of systems. Instead of being one phase near the end of a development effort, implementation is used to

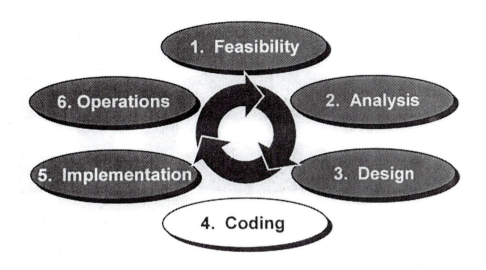

FIGURE 8-1. The system development life cycle.

describe the overall process in which development of software may or may not be one phase.

A number of factors have contributed to the inversion of the SDLC. Part of the motivation away from the SDLC has come from recognition of the technical limitations of the code-centric view of information systems. Many other technical dimensions of applications—such as data and databases, networks and communications infrastructures—are becoming as prominent as software.

A more significant influence on how information systems are built is the growing recognition of the importance of the organizational context in which they are used. As a small phase in traditional development, implementation has comprised those trivial activities related to putting the system in its organizational setting. We now know that these activities are not trivial at all and, in fact, are critical to the success of most systems-building efforts. Finally, we now recognize that information systems are not purely technical, but that organizations—their processes, people, and structures—are an integral part of any information system.

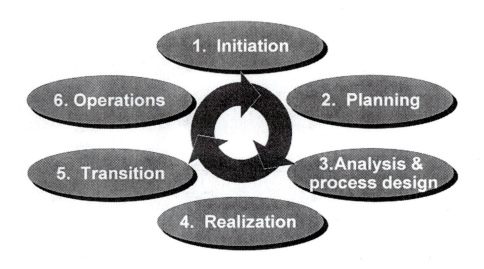

FIGURE 8-2. Enterprise system implementation phases.

Enterprise systems implementation is thus as much organizational engineering as it is software engineering. It involves taking a stock technical solution, customizing that solution to the organizational setting, and adapting the organization and its processes to the system. This requires a large investment in planning and a genuine understanding of the organizational setting.

Major Phases of Enterprise System Implementation

Although described differently by different authors, software vendors, and consulting firms, enterprise system implementation consists of a set of phases (Figure 8-2) similar to the following.

1. Initiation—This is the phase in which the business case for the implementation is made, as well as major decisions about the project scope and implementation strategy. Also, this phase usually includes the selection of methodology, software and hardware vendors, and consulting partners.

2. Planning—The planning phase is focused on setting up the project administration, determining the staffing arrangements, setting goals

and objectives, acquiring resources, and establishing metrics for the implementation project.

3. Analysis and process design—This phase involves analyzing the organization and its current processes, redesigning those processes as needed, and creating a mapping from the organization "as is" to the organization "to be."

4. Realization—The realization phase entails installing a base system, customizing it to the organization, extending it if necessary, and testing the implementation.

5. Transition—This is usually a relatively short phase during which the organization's former information systems are replaced with the enterprise system.

6. Operation—The operation phase involves ongoing efforts to monitor system performance and tune the system as appropriate. It also involves the continuing process of training employees on the enterprise system.

Initiating an Implementation Project

The initiation phase of an enterprise system implementation project is critical because it establishes the foundation for all that follows. It begins by building the business case for the system, which is essential for obtaining senior management buy-in for the project. Next, a number of major decisions about the implementation project need to be made, including scope and strategy, methodology, software and hardware vendors, and consulting partners. These decisions become cornerstones for the project charter, which is a high-level initial project-planning document.

Building the Business Case: The Project Charter

The business case for the enterprise system implementation, also known as the project charter, initiates or starts the project. The main components of the business case are:

■ The mission of the project or the main goals.

■ Project objectives or measurable desired outcomes.

■ Business drivers or the environmental forces that are driving the organization to do the implementation project.

■ Issues, barriers, or restraining forces that may inhibit the project's success.

- Project measures or how the organization knows when the project is completed and/or how the project is making progress.

Since the business case has been developed prior to initiation of the project, the issues surrounding the feasibility of the enterprise system should have been addressed. The areas of feasibility that get revisited during the initiation phase are: technical, organizational, and economic. For example, the project and business drivers are similar to the economic feasibility factors addressed in the business case. Similarly, barriers and issues that surface during the initiation phase are similar to concerns about the technical and organizational feasibility. For example, how much change the organization can tolerate at one time may be highly dependent on the organizational culture surrounding change. In organizations that are resistant to change, certain issues or barriers to enterprise system implementation make it less organizationally feasible than in organizations that have a culture that encourages or embraces change. Typically (but not always), large organizations that have been in business for more than 25 years are more resistant to changes imposed by enterprise systems than organizations that are younger.

Determining the Scope and Strategy

Once the project charter has been developed, the organization needs to review the implementation strategy. Basically, there are four types of enterprise systems implementation projects:

1. Initial implementations where there is no organizational history of an enterprise system.
2. Subsequent rollouts of the initial or core system in other business areas or geographic locations within the same organization.
3. Upgrades to the existing system.
4. Enhancement projects where new functional areas or modules are added to the core system.

Within each of these types of implementations there are also strategies that range from a basically top-down approach such as blueprinting to a bottom-up approach that is essentially driven by legacy system data needs.

Blueprinting

This top-down strategy involves looking at the processes within the enterprise system and finding the subset that best represents how the corporation wants to do business. Once these processes are identified, then the business compares the "as is" situation (how they currently do business) with the "to be" processes, or the chosen functionality from the enterprise system. Where the "as is" diverges from the "to be," there are two basic choices: either change the business to conform to the enterprise system processes or change the enterprise system to fit the business. Since the decision to use a third-party system is made with the idea that the company is outsourcing the development of the enterprise system, changing the software (except within ERP-vendor prescribed limits) is discouraged. Companies that have modified the original source code find that upgrades are more difficult, if not impossible, and the loss of keeping their own system current has major disadvantages. Companies that have success in getting the enterprise system to a place of core support of the business have rigid rules for code modification and minimize the changes as much as possible (Chevron, Standard Oil, Bay Networks).

Bottom-Up Data-Driven Approach

This strategy is designed to minimize the changes to the current business environment by mapping the existing data elements into the database of the enterprise system. All of the enterprise system processes are more or less accepted as applying to some part of the business, and instead of modifying the business to fit the enterprise system, the company tries to map the existing data needs to the enterprise system tables. Generally, this involves some customization of reports and data manipulation so that the processes of the business can remain as is. The risk associated with this approach is that the corporate definitions of data elements may not map exactly to those definitions provided by the enterprise system developer and some of the linkages in the database can be "broken," reducing the effectiveness of the enterprise system as a true enterprise solution. However, the impact on the business is less severe, and in the case of financial information the basic needs of the corporation can be met with this approach.

IMPLEMENTATION CHECKLIST #1

REVIEW IMPLEMENTATION STRATEGY

- ☐ Will this strategy work?
- ☐ What would you change about it?
- ☐ What is missing that you would include?
- ☐ What is included that is not needed?
- ☐ What are the key assumptions?

Of course, there are variations of each of these approaches, and to some extent corporations use a little of each. If the bottom-up approach dominates, then the corporation must be careful to document the mapping process and identify the corporate data names as they are used within the enterprise system. If the blueprinting approach is used, then the corporation needs to be clear on how the current processes need to change since people tend to use the new system in old ways.

Big Bang versus Phased Approach

Another decision that must be made is whether or not to implement everything (all the targeted functionality) as one implementation project or to phase in the functionality by module or submodule. For example, let's assume the company has decided to support the business in the financial and material management areas first. The company is largely a distribution business, and it wants to implement the core process of material management or movement of goods to/from inventory as well as the related financial modules for external reporting. Let's also assume the company is global and operates in several different locations throughout the world. The decision to separate the implementation into geographic phases is made so that separate database servers can support processing at key times that fit the local work time periods. Geographic separation also allows for testing to conform to local tax and legal requirements and for the management of change issues to be localized. Given this (already phased approach by geography), the decision still remains: Shall we implement all the modules in this geography as one project (big bang), or shall we break the project into modular phases?

The case for the big bang approach is that in configuring and testing an enterprise system the modules are integrated, meaning that the modules share data and processes. Thus, a certain efficiency and effectiveness are achieved by implementing the modules as one project. For example, in SAP's R/3 system, tables for banks, document types, messages to customers and vendors, payment terms, and so on, are shared by procurement (in the material management module), accounts receivable, accounts payable, and the general ledger. If each of these modules is implemented separately, then there is a chance that configuration changes may be made along the way that conflict with previous settings. In the big bang approach, all the process experts must agree to the configuration settings up front, requiring a more integrated approach to implementation. On the other hand, there is less overall testing because the modules can share test data, and there is less risk that one process team can overwrite the settings made by another team.

Another advantage of the big bang approach is that the teams learn to work together, which can break down traditional bureaucratic functional silos evident in many large corporations. Teams learn about the intermodular functionality from the beginning and can start the change to a more enterprise way of thinking (and behaving). If one of the business drivers is the standardization of processes, then getting the process experts from the different functional areas to work together early in the project can amount to process gains as the group explores ways to jointly meet their individual requirements. Teamwork can be used to break down the traditional silos that exist in many large global organizations.

The case for separation of the modules into separate implementations is that the projects are more homogeneous in nature, less disruptive to the business in general, and easier to manage. Since they require less coordination up front and the projects are easier to manage, the implementations seem to move along more quickly than in the big bang approach. One danger in lengthy implementations is that user buy-in wanes because the project takes a long time. People begin to think that the enterprise system will never happen, and they behave accordingly. Most failures in organizational change are due to "social inertia" (Keen, 1981),

IMPLEMENTATION CHECKLIST #2

CONFIRM IMPLEMENTATION METHODOLOGY

- ☐ Will this methodology and these phases work for this implementation?
- ☐ What would you change?
- ☐ What is missing that you would include?
- ☐ What is included that is not needed?
- ☐ What are the key assumptions?

and certainly long enterprise system implementations are guilty of social inertia. ("Social inertia" is defined as trying hard to make something happen while things stay the same.) As people see success in small chunks, the project seems to be progressing and users see tangible results more quickly. At the same time, the tendency to maintain functional silos is easier in the more modular approach, and less organizational change is evident as the project moves through smaller steps that preserve the modular tendency of the business.

This tendency to maintain functional silos is evident in many ways, not the least of which is the use of reconciliation or suspense accounts in accounting so that the module can stand alone until the other modules are implemented. For example, if accounts payable is used to acquire assets but the asset module is not implemented, the purchase cannot post directly to a fixed asset, giving it value. Rather, the purchase posts to a general ledger (GL) account for assets in general or to a suspense account until the posting can be moved to an assigned asset. After both the payables and asset modules are implemented along with the GL, then integration among the modules can be achieved. (At this time, however, it is likely that people in the organization will need to change in order to break down the stand-alone aspects of the system that were put in place during the piecemeal implementation project.)

Many organizations use a combination of these methods such as a big bang approach within a geography-based or phased approach by module. The extremes are big bang of all modules for the whole organization (applicable to organizations with few global differences) to modular phase-in by geography. In either case, changes to the system through customization, configuration, and code revision to meet local needs should be tightly controlled, documented, and monitored. Code changes should only be allowed with an approved documented business case, and all code changes should be coordinated centrally.

In general then, the advantages of one approach are disadvantages in the other approach, and each organization must weigh the costs and benefits given their business case driving the enterprise system. If standard processes that are integrated is the overall driving factor, then the case for a big bang approach is more compelling than if the driving factor is replacement of many legacy systems into one seamless application.

Choosing a Project Methodology

Choices are as numerous as enterprise system implementation partners and organizations using the enterprise system. Choices usually include the adaptation of the corporate project methodology to an enterprise system implementation project, using a methodology from the implementation partner, such as Accenture, and Cap Gemini E&Y Consulting, or a methodology provided by the ERP supplier, such as Accelerated SAP or the R/3 procedure model. Many of the methodologies offered by implementation partners are derived from models developed by ERP vendors, with modifications based on the partners' experience with the products.

Selecting Platforms and Vendors

Some ERP vendors and third-party providers are beginning to bundle software with hardware. Examples are solutions by Pandesic (a now defunct joint venture of SAP and Intel), and DataWorks, which bundles the desired enterprise system (SAP, Oracle applications, or PeopleSoft) with the Microsoft platform (Horner, 1998). SAP has a product call RRR (Ready to Run R/3) that has SAP's R/3 preloaded and preconfigured on different hardware platforms such as HP, Dell, and Sun. It is targeted for the smaller business and is designed to get companies up and running more quickly.

Most hardware vendors have partnered with the major ERP providers to have specification programs and infrastructure specifications that work with the ERP product. So once an organization selects an ERP vendor, the hardware company can specify (and sell) the needed hardware to run the chosen software. HP, IBM, Dell, and Sun all have implementation services surrounding the infrastructure component selection processes.

The technical area of needs assessment includes hardware specification, assessment of the network infrastructure, and determination of desktop needs. Some enterprise systems require more "power" on the desktop than others, and hopefully when the product was chosen, this assessment was completed so that there are few surprises during this phase of the implementation. Support needs and post go-live service levels need to be determined and specified so that planning can begin.

Another key issue that needs to be assessed during this phase is security requirements. Design criteria and organizational standards need to be applied to the security requirements of the chosen enterprise system. Naming conventions for the security system and coming up with a way to test end-user IDs and passwords need to be developed.

Finally, a development system needs to be acquired, installed, and secured so that upon completion of the gap analysis by the project team, design and development can begin without delay. This is no small task because the development system needs to have access to the network infrastructure, printing network, and systems administration procedures. The security design needs to be tested and implemented prior to design so that developers can test user authorizations and development ideas on a real system.

In most cases, the vendor that the organization has chosen to provide the hardware helps with the assessment and requirements definition. IBM, Hewlett-Packard, Compaq, Dell, and the like all have enterprise system specification tools that take data about the organization and determine what size of system is needed for production, testing, and development. The chosen vendor can also help define the backup and recovery strategies that need to be in place to ensure that the system stays up when needed and can recover from any unplanned failure.

Opting for a Project Partner

In 1998 Gartner Group surveyed businesses that had implemented or were planning to implement an enterprise system. They found that about 66.2 percent of the companies preferred to use an implementation partner from the ERP vendor. The perceived advantages were that the vendor had the most knowledge about the product that was chosen and could summon the best resources when facing implementation issues. Those companies that preferred non-ERP vendors (16.9 percent) believe that independent vendors have a better understanding of the full range of implementation issues and can be more flexible in solving problems. The remaining 16.9 percent don't have a preference as to choice of vendor.

The market for implementation partners is at least three times the ERP software market. For example, in 1998 the professional services market related to enterprise systems was $25.4 billion, and by 2003 it is expected to be $97 billion (Diederich, 1999). Only about 15 percent of these services are supplied by the ERP vendors themselves, with the rest of the demand being met by the Big Five accounting firms, smaller providers like Sapient and EDS, and the hardware vendors, such as IBM, Hewlett-Packard, and Compaq (Datamation).

With rapid growth in the enterprise system market, expertise in specific ERP products by all consulting partners and ERP vendors has been in short supply (to one extent or another) since about 1995. As the ERP vendors and consulting companies expand their ranks to meet the demand, it is possible to get less experience than desired from either type of partner. This author has sat in more than one training class where other students in the class (who worked for consulting companies and the ERP vendor) were leaving the class on Friday in order to enter into a consulting engagement the following Monday where they were the "expert." Companies that have had experiences with less than expected expertise have fairly detailed contracts with the consultants (independent or vendor specific), specifying the level of expertise required for their project.

Summary

In this chapter we examined enterprise systems implementation from a very high level. We began with a discussion of how information systems are built, and we pointed out some key differences between traditional systems development and enterprise systems implementation. We explained that, by treating an enterprise system implementation as just another IT project, many companies neglect the fact that these systems change organizations in fundamental ways. After the reviewing all phases of enterprise system implementation, the chapter focused on the first phase: initiation and the creation of the project charter.

Discussion Questions

1. What does the word "implementation" mean in a traditional software development project compared to an enterprise system implementation project?

2. What does the author mean by "turning the life cycle inside out"?

3. What are the major phases or processes for an enterprise system implementation project? What is the purpose of each?

4. How is an enterprise system's blueprint similar to blueprints used to build a house? How is it different?

5. Give an example of both a big bang approach and a phased approach to implementing enterprise systems.

6. If a large global enterprise decides to roll out the financial module, the material or inventory management module and production scheduling and execution in projects within each of five operating concerns, what constitutes a big bang approach? a phased approach?

7. List the major advantages and disadvantages of a big bang approach compared to a phased approach.

8. Trade articles talk about the importance of project management methods and managers to the success of enterprise system implementation. What is a project management method? Why is it important? What is more important, the method or the manager? Defend your choice.

9. What are the most important factors to consider in choosing a hardware platform provider, partner or vendor?

10. What is the project charter? How is it used through the enterprise system implementation project?

References

___, "Implementing ERP: Desperately Seeking SAP Support." Datamation, August 12, 1998.

Diederich, Tom. "ERP Vendors Will Focus on Services." Computerworld, April 12, 1999.

Gartner Group. "ERP and FMIS Study." Multi-client study, November 1998.

Horner, Peter. "DataWorks CEO Envisions Growth, Changes in Mid-Range ERP." *www.lionhrtpub.com/ee/ee-spring98/dataworksqa.html*

Keen, Peter G.W. "Information Systems and Organizational Change." *Communications of the ACM* 24, no. 1 (January 1981): 24–33.

Chapter 9

The Design of Enterprise Systems

For every complex problem, there is a solution that is simple, neat, and wrong. — H. L. Mencken

mong the factors associated with successful enterprise systems implementation projects is thorough planning and design. Much of this activity takes place long before any computer hardware and software is installed and configured, any data is transferred, or any users are trained on the system. More than anything else, the planning and design phases help to prepare an organization for the significant changes that implementing an enterprise system entails.

OBJECTIVES

- Describe the planning phase of enterprise system implementation.

- Explore the analysis and design of organizational processes.

- Demonstrate key questions, tasks, and decisions facing implementers.

This chapter continues the exploration of enterprise system implementation from the point immediately following the project initiation phase (see Figure 9-1). While it is assumed that the organization and specifically its top management have made a commitment to the

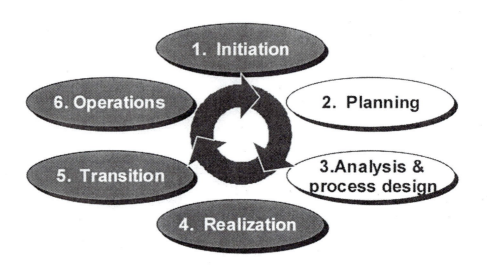

FIGURE 9-1. Selected enterprise system implementation phases.

project by this time, much of the administrative detail must still be developed. The first part of the chapter deals with these planning tasks, including: creating the project administration, assembling the project staff, setting goals and objectives, developing project resources, and establishing project metrics.

Even before these planning activities are complete, the project moves into its next phase: analyzing and (re)designing the enterprise. The purpose of this phase is to carefully match the generic organizational processes encoded in the software and data of the selected enterprise system with the actual processes of the organization. This is achieved through three steps: (1) uncovering existing processes, (2) creating a set of ideal processes, (3) and performing an analysis of differences between these two sets of processes.

Throughout the chapter, implementation checklists are intended to provide a sense of some of the key questions, tasks, and decisions that face enterprise system implementation managers and staff.

DEFINE OR CONFIRM STANDARDS AND PROCEDURES

Define or validate the major components of the communication plan (areas or levels of information about which different people need to be kept informed, i.e., project plans, budgets, major milestones and/or show stoppers, routine project status, issues, and/or day-to-day activities).

☐ Who needs to be on the contact list for each component in the plan?

☐ How should the contact list be informed? (voice, e-mail, formal report, post to web site, etc.)

☐ How often should the contact list be informed?

☐ What standards need to be followed to document the project, the system, and the processes?

☐ What Project Standards and Procedures exist from prior projects that we want to use here?

Planning an Implementation Project

One of the last steps in the initiation phase is to commence the project with a formal kickoff meeting. At this meeting, high-level planning begins to take shape. Details about project administration, staffing, refined milestones and objectives, resources, and project metrics are formalized in the planning phase.

Creating the Project Administration

Perhaps the most important part of planning the enterprise system implementation involves project management and administration. Having the right project team, especially the project manager, is critical to the success of the project. Choosing the project methodology and having someone from the company who can manage a project plan are very important. In the Chevron case study that follows, for example, project

IMPLEMENTATION CHECKLIST #4

DETERMINE THE CHANGE CONTROL PROCESS

This process may already exist in the organization and just needs to be confirmed or refined for the project. But this should not be distributed to the process teams—it needs to be centralized for the organization. The change control process needs to include at least the following:

- ☐ A method to track open issues for this project.
- ☐ Identification of existing standards for change control.
- ☐ A definition and method to assign levels of priority and status to each issue.

When an issue represents potential for a change in either the business process or the system:

- ☐ What is the process for introducing the change?
- ☐ What approval process needs to be followed?
- ☐ What signoff criteria are needed to ensure that QA procedures are followed?

management was named one of the most critical success factors in SAP R/3 implementation.

Project Administration includes finding the right project manager at a high enough level to make decisions and changes quickly. This person needs to have the full authority of top management to drive the project to completion on time.

IMPLEMENTATION CHECKLIST #5

ESTABLISH PROJECT TEAM WORKING ENVIRONMENT

- ☐ Validate stakeholders and impacted organizations (make sure they are part of the team).
- ☐ Determine location and needed infrastructure of project office.

REFINE PROJECT ORGANIZATION AND ROLES (AND RESPONSIBILITIES)

Most methodologies have a predefined set of Roles and Responsibilities. We need to validate those roles and see if the project scope dictates the elimination or consolidation of roles.

- ☐ What roles are needed to assure project success? (Describe in as much detail as desired.)
- ☐ What are the responsibilities for each role?
- ☐ Do we need to prioritize responsibilities?
- ☐ What are the criteria for selecting people to be assigned to a role? (i.e., length of time in the job, reporting relationships, team player, etc.)

Associated with developing the appropriate project team environment is assessing the risks and developing controls so that barriers to implementation can be addressed in a timely, cost-effective manner. Formal risk assessment is part of this process where key managers from affected areas of the business identify the likely risks and can help develop controls to mitigate those risks. Risk assessment needs to address technical issues as well as business issues.

Finally, in addition to technical, project, and business issues, a team of people on the project needs to look at the change management issues that the enterprise system implementation is likely to raise. Change management includes everything from how to manage the versions of software changes in the technical environment to how to manage the behavioral change required of end users. By far the harder of these extremes is how to manage the impact on people in the organization.

To get the most benefit from the integrated aspects of enterprise systems, there may be significant requirements to change the current business model or processes. Changing the business processes means that people in the organization need to do some or all things differently. Change management

IMPLEMENTATION CHECKLIST #7

ASSIGN/COMMIT PEOPLE TO ROLES

- ☐ Given each role, identify candidates within the organization to fill each role.
- ☐ Vote on the most appropriate candidate where more than one is named.
- ☐ Define and select options/alternatives to fill the holes (places where no one is identified).

involves understanding where the behavioral and technical changes are likely, who is affected, and a plan to manage the changes and their affects.

Assembling the Project Staff

The composition of the project team is critical to the success of enterprise system implementation projects. Among the common roles are:

IMPLEMENTATION CHECKLIST #8

DETERMINE KNOWLEDGE TRANSFER (KT) NEEDS

Once we know who the key players are, we can identify the knowledge or expertise that may be needed to successfully execute the project.

- ☐ What expertise/knowledge areas are needed in order to assure a successful implementation?

For each of these areas:

- ☐ Who or what role(s) needs the expertise?
- ☐ What sources can we use to meet the need?
- ☐ What is the best way to extract and transfer the needed knowledge or expertise to those who need it? (i.e., group training, CBT, training the trainer, documentation, etc.)

IMPLEMENTATION CHECKLIST #9

DEFINE PROJECT DRIVERS

- ☐ Start with a list of factors in the business case, add to the list, and comment on the existing list.
- ☐ Rate each item with respect to strength. (How strong is each of these drivers?) This activity provides the project with overall guidance in how to prioritize conflicting initiatives as the project gets underway.

- A manager with proven project management experience.
- Solution experts who know the ERP package, its functionality, and related implementation issues.
- Business process experts who know the business at least in the functional areas being considered for the project scope.
- Technical experts in the areas of (1) system-to-system interfaces (both inbound and outbound), (2) current system data, especially in the systems that are targets for replacement by the enterprise system, and (3) database, network, and operating system expertise for the environment supporting the enterprise system.
- Geographic business process experts who know the legal, tax, and currency rules/issues that may arise by using the chosen enterprise system in different geographies. For example, many non-U.S. countries have legal rules regarding bad debt writeoffs, invoicing, document retention standards, and credit terms that must be applied by companies operating within their borders. Non-U.S. countries have taxes on inventory, invoices, and services that do not conform to rules of business in the United States. In general, one advantage of ERP products is that they conform to these tax and legal rules in different countries, but not every ERP package supports the rules in every country and principality in which the company may operate.
- Change management experts who can identify potential change management issues for technical version control, but also those who can help prepare the end-user community for the process changes that may affect the way they perform future work tasks using the enterprise system. This includes site readiness issue identification and planning,

DRIVING THE ERP HIGHWAY:
CHEVRON CORPORATION AND SAP

You may not realize this, but every time you fill your gas tank at a Chevron, you are helping to reengineer a company—a vast, $43 billion, Fortune 100 company that is the eighth largest producer of petroleum and chemical products—an organization that just seven years ago relied on over two hundred separate mainframe systems, like little islands operating in a sea of confusion. When Chevron merged with Gulf Corporation in the late 1980s, the already unwieldy mass of information the company was struggling to organize made the snarl nearly impossible to manage. Something had to be done about the computer systems before Chevron truly began to suffer financial and informational losses.

In 1990, CFO Marty Klitten undertook a study that ultimately made a very compelling case for making significant changes in Chevron's financial systems. He assembled a core team for the project, dubbed AFIS (Advanced Financial Information Systems), and they began a project plan. First, they determined the scope and cost of the project, and found that the annual cost of the current systems was over $100 million. The team also decided that implementing new process systems could save them at least $25 million annually. As for the expected cost of the project, they set the figure between $80 million and $100 million.

Then it was time to choose a vendor. Chevron was interested in finding a vendor with a large enough infrastructure to support the conglomerate and finally decided on SAP. Chevron felt that going with SAP would enable it to limit the modifications of its current work processes. One of the challenges to both Chevron and SAP was how to integrate the new systems when Chevron

was really a conglomeration of 12 different operating companies. Part of its systems implementation strategy was to begin the changes within two of the smaller companies, Warren Petroleum and Chevron Pipeline Company. Then it would work its way up to the larger, higher-risk companies within Chevron. Thus the AFIS team began to work on the first of their three rollouts.

The AFIS core team, together with SAP, decided that the best way to manage the large number of operating companies was to group them together based on characteristics they shared in common. Then they decided that within each "grouping" employees had to be given a standard training course to keep them abreast of the changes taking place in the corporation. The team also developed a common business process design across the entire corporation. In addition, they came up with a step-by-step methodology to manage the corporate project. Members of the core AFIS team acted as consultants to the Chevron companies, helping them to design processes and facilitate the changes that were taking place.

The gradual rollouts Chevron has been implementing in the last few years have produced many benefits for the corporation. Strategically, data accuracy has improved significantly and is much more manageable for the average employee to view and understand. Managers have greater access to the financial status of their areas and are better able to make changes in purchasing and cost information without having to travel through an unwieldy maze of data. Chevron anticipates that it is saving even more annually in information systems costs, up to $50 million.

With all of the positives achieved by implementing ERP, Chevron also learned some important lessons. The project was even larger than initially anticipated, with costs ballooning to over $100 million. This was partly due to the fact that Chevron underestimated the number of users of the new systems. In fact, the corporation notes that in the long term, more users of the system exist outside the financial area than within it.

In addition, the role played by the AFIS core team ended up being significantly larger in both scale and complexity than initially planned. Yet another costly endeavor involved upgrades to the SAP software, for which Chevron had not planned. They had hoped, as will be recalled, to come out of the implementation with few changes to their work processes; but in the long term they realized that they wanted to make some modifications for future benefits to Chevron.

Today Chevron is still pumping in benefits from adopting an ERP system. The company attributes the success of the project to the core AFIS team, the common process designs, methodologies, training, its executive sponsorships, and its rollout plan, which called for a slow but steady approach to change.

training needs assessment and deployment, and the execution of tactical plans designed to overcome the resistance to change likely to be encountered after the go-live date.

Setting Goals and Objectives

Identify Business Drivers

What are the driving business factors that move the organization into an enterprise system implementation? How can each of these driving factors best be realized? For example, if standardizing processes across a diverse and decentralized organization is the driving factor for obtaining an enterprise system, then the processes (as is) need to be fully understood so that a replacement standard process can be found that minimizes the overall organizational change and maximizes the likelihood that the corporation can use one standard process in every operating location. If the driving factor is replacement of a few fragmented legacy systems, then finding the best fit of processes within the enterprise system that are being replaced is a key decision component. In short, it is important that the implementation process demonstrate that it can deliver on the key business reasons for

IMPLEMENTATION CHECKLIST #10

DEFINE PROJECT RESTRAINING FORCES

☐ Build a list of restraining factors. If included in the business case or risk assessment that is typically done prior to the implementation project, start with these.

☐ Rate each item with respect to strength. (How strong is each of these restraining forces—that may keep the project from succeeding?)

☐ Make these items the starting point for a change management implementation plan. Use the drivers to overcome the restrainers wherever possible.

acquiring the enterprise system. If the enterprise system can add value over and above the business case factors, then the implementation has some added benefits, but the implementation strategy must be able to deliver on its business case promises. This is important because most large system implementations go through a renewed commitment to the project when it is learned that the implementation will take longer and cost more than originally planned (Corbitt, Norman, and Butler, 1994).

Both Chevron and Hewlett-Packard are companies that started out on an enterprise system project and about halfway through reassessed whether the investment was worth the effort. In each of these cases, a second business case was developed that showed the progress being made in achieving the original business case drivers and finding more benefits in pursuing the project. Ironically, each of these companies found major financial benefits in the quality of data offered by the Asset management module in the enterprise system. Chevron documented $30 million savings in taxes the first year alone through better asset management.

Developing Project Resources

After the goals and project team members have been identified, budget and resource plans can be developed. These plans start out at a high level where dollars are assigned to major categories of expense such as knowledge transfer (includes training, documentation, etc.), project management,

IMPLEMENTATION CHECKLIST #11

CREATE BUDGET AND RESOURCE PLANS

- ☐ Define or verify the major categories of expenses related to the implementation.
- ☐ Assign dollars to each category.
- ☐ Define and assign sources for resources for each category.
- ☐ Focus on categories where resources have not been identified (i.e., infrastructure, travel, etc.).
- ☐ Be creative in defining resources that can meet the needed expense(s) within each category.

software, and hardware. Knowing the in-house people determines the cost of the internal people resource.

Most companies also contract with consulting and implementation partners, and these costs are needed for the resource plan as well. In the first implementations of an enterprise system, consulting companies had contracts that were process driven where companies paid for services. With smaller implementations and now that there is more experience in contracting for implementation services, the trend is toward fixed price contracts that are outcomes-driven. For example, a company may contract with a consulting firm at a fixed fee to manage the project or for the delivery of a tested security system.

Estimating costs and determining the sources for the needed resources often present a challenge, especially for firms with no prior experience in rolling out a major system that can touch nearly every aspect of the organization. But commitment to the plan is required, so budget and resource planning are important to the success of the rest of the project. Companies need adequate resources to embark on an enterprise system implementation project.

Establishing Project Metrics

As the project begins, another important aspect of project management is to determine the measures both for the actual progress of the project

IMPLEMENTATION CHECKLIST #12

IDENTIFY BUSINESS MEASURES

- [ ] Start with a list in business case (measures of business success).
- [ ] Verify that each measure is truly measurable—what is the measure now?
- [ ] Prioritize measures by importance to the success of the organization. (This can be used to trade off conflicting situations that may arise during the course of the project.)

compared to the project plan and for the achievement of business objectives. Articles that discuss enterprise system implementation success indicate that having a solid business case and showing that the business case is coming true are important project indicators. This means that the project plan needs to include measurable outcomes and milestones along the way. It is necessary to show the progress that has been made and to demonstrate that the desired outcomes to the business are in fact being met.

Answering the basic question, "How do we know the project is finished?" is important. Having both business and project measures to show progress may be the momentum that keeps the project on track at critical times and keeps the project motivated to meet deadlines. If the users of the enterprise system cannot see measurable progress and change toward meeting the stated goals, the environment can become very unhealthy and key people may leave the organization.

IMPLEMENTATION CHECKLIST #13

IDENTIFY PROJECT MEASURES

- [ ] What factors can be used to measure project success (i.e., stay within budget, deliver on time, engage stakeholders, deliver specified functionality)?
- [ ] How can we measure each?
- [ ] When or how often should each be measured?
- [ ] What are the tradeoffs (which are most important)?

Analyzing and (Re)designing the Enterprise

The analysis phase of the implementation process is one of the most critical. Companies learn what they know and don't know about their own business. The major activities within this phase are to capture the current situation of the business, determine what the ideal state is with the enterprise system in place, and then conduct a gap analysis. The current situation is known as the "as is" picture and the future enterprise system state is known as the "to be" picture.

Uncovering the "As Is" Picture—Analyzing Existing Processes

Business Process Needs Assessment

The major areas of business process needs assessment include the following:

- Refine the project scope. (What functional areas are included in each cycle of the project rollout?)
- Define both configuration standards and a process for coordinating the setup of the system to support the functional areas within scope. For example, in SAP's R/3, some configuration settings are shared across modules, so that each area needs to define what settings rely on input from other process areas (such as bank information, document type definition, etc.) and what settings can be done independently.
- Determine what types of users are included within each process area so that the security design developed by the technical team can be tested and validated. The security system needs to model the business processes and have the ability to change as the business changes.
- Determine the information requirements (reports, queries, etc.) for each functional area by type of user.
- Determine the process requirements. (What kinds of processes are needed to support the business, and what business rules must each follow to meet the needs of the business for internal as well as external reporting?)
- Define the organization structure and map this structure to that assumed by the enterprise system. For example, SAP uses company codes, plants, sales organizations, and so on, in very specific ways, and

each organization that uses R/3 needs to map the structural elements in SAP's R/3 to the organization.

■ Determine the required interfaces with existing or legacy systems both for the purposes of one-time conversion (if the existing system is to be replaced by the enterprise system) and interfacing for those systems that support functionality outside the scope of the current implementation project.

Change Management Requirements

Change management efforts at this point in the project include an analysis of the business drivers and restraining factors identified in the project charter. The change management team may need to develop a site readiness plan that looks at not only the technical changes that need to take place but also the likelihood of behavioral changes that are required as the new system's processes are implemented. This group may also be responsible for coordinating the results of the needs assessment to the organization as a whole and for providing team-building support for the existing teams.

The change management team also coordinates and develops the knowledge transfer plan as it affects the project team. In other words, the project team may require some training in the enterprise system's functional or technical areas. These efforts need to be coordinated so that all training areas are covered by some part of the implementation team.

Creating the "To Be" Picture—Business Process Redesign

Business process reengineering (BPR) was introduced in Chapter 4. But even if one has a good conceptual grasp of BPR, this does not mean that one can actually perform BPR. Many methods can be used to create the "to be" picture, but regardless of the method chosen, all methods share some common elements for doing BPR or BPR-like processes. These elements include the notion of customer focus, and the outcomes of the process have to be the value received by the customers or stakeholders of the process.

Another common element is that a cross-functional team is required so that everyone can understand all aspects of each major business process. Finally, all the methods involve a phased approach that can be outlined in four to six steps, including the following:

1. Assess the customer-driven objectives of the process; what does the customer receive from the process that has value?
2. Map or define the current process.
3. Analyze the current process by identifying the candidates for reengineering or redesign. (Perform an in-depth analysis identifying all the places in the current process where improvements can be made.)
4. Redesign or reengineer the prime candidates. (Focus on those places in the process, or whole processes, where you can get the most value to the customer for the least cost or effort.)
5. Implement and evaluate the impact on the customer.

Some methods add a gap analysis phase in which the process as it should be or could be is compared to the process as it is to ascertain where the largest gaps exist, but this phase can be subsumed within the analysis phase of the project. Other methods add benchmarking as part of analysis as well so that companies can compare what they do with "best of breed."

Nearly all authors agree that implementation is the area in which BPR projects are most likely to fail. This is because change, no matter how large or small, needs to be managed within all organizations and the management of change unfortunately receives little attention until things start to go badly.

With enterprise systems, BPR has a dual role—one of result and the other as a prerequisite. Therefore, enterprise systems can actually be the mechanism or catalyst for achieving process improvements that the organization wants to make. In this sense, the enterprise system is the enabler, making BPR happen within an organization. At Chevron, for example, there were two failed attempts to implement process changes in the company. Management finally decided that if it changed the information system, the process improvements it wanted would result from enterprise system implementation. In this case, the company goes into the enterprise system implementation knowing that process improvements are an outcome.

When using the enterprise system to facilitate business process improvements, the following assumptions are made:

1. Automation supports the value to the customer. (In other words, by fully automating the processes, the customer is better off.)

2. Processes within the enterprise system need continuous improvement, and so the organization implementing the enterprise system wants to take advantage of new functionality in upgrades.
3. Management needs to be lean.
4. The ERP vendor knows what best of breed practices and/or processes are and have included them in the system.

By including the process improvements from the enterprise system into the business and making the business change if necessary in order to take advantage of the enterprise system processes, the company is minimizing custom changes to the enterprise system. This allows the company to use the enterprise system as delivered and enhances its ability to use new functionality that is released by the ERP vendor.

In other cases, BPR is a prerequisite to enterprise system implementation, or at least process changes are made during the implementation phase. This is typical in an accelerated implementation of the enterprise system where process changes need to be in place and little customization is done to the software during implementation. When BPR is done prior to or during enterprise system implementation, the software processes are understood prior to implementation. In this way, choices can be made as to the best way to reengineer the business ahead of time.

Analyzing the Gaps

During the gap analysis phase in the implementation process the "as is" situation—the current environment before enterprise system—is compared to the "to be" situation. "To be" is determined by the requirements analysis and indicates what the processes will look like after the enterprise system is implemented. If a phased approach to implementation is used, a separate gap analysis is sometimes performed for each separate portion of the enterprise system implementation. The only drawback to this more piecemeal approach is that some key integration components may get overlooked.

Two basic questions are being asked during the gap analysis regardless of project scope:
1. Where does the organization need to change in order to take advantage of the enterprise system functionality?

2. Where does the enterprise system need to change in order to meet the unique functionality required by the organization?

More and more, the emphasis is on the first question, changing the organization rather than changing the enterprise system. Companies that were eager to change the enterprise system found the upgrade and testing issues to be significant. To make changing the organization more attractive, ERP vendors frequently release new product versions, adding in the functionality that companied want. Since updates can come out once or twice a year, the wait for added functionality compared to the added time to test custom changes against the new release can make changing the organization more attractive.

On the other hand, changing an organization is no small task. Change management was considered a major success factor in the Chevron implementation, and the lack of managed methods for changing an organization's processes is often attributed to enterprise system implementation failure.

At the end of the analysis phase, or the gap analysis phase in the generic scenario, decisions have been made about the following:

- Specific requirements for processes within scope for the baseline or initial cycle of the implementation.
- The way to configure or implement the organizational structure within the enterprise system's structural components.
- Required interfaces, conversions, and enhancements needed to meet the unique needs of the organization.
- Master data requirements. (What data elements are mandatory and optional in order to meet the needs of the organization?)
- Change management needs such as training and procedural changes for end users of the required processes.

Summary

It is important that all key players in the implementation participate in the kickoff meeting so that the team will know the seriousness of the ERP project at hand. After the kickoff more in-depth planning takes place that refines the scope, determines project team requirements, and develops a detailed project plan.

The work of starting the implementation project really gets going in the analysis phase. Members of the project team representing functional business areas, technology specialties, and organizational change management are busy defining the current environment. The team gathers requirements that form the basis of the planned system and end with a gap analysis that compares the "as is" to the "to be" system. This gap analysis becomes the basis for the detailed work to follow (discussed in Chapter 10). It is important that all three groups of people examine the gaps from their own unique perspective.

Discussion Questions

1. If the three main groups of project team members come from technology, business process and change management areas, discuss the relative importance of each group and the ideal kinds of people you'd like to have on the project team.

2. The Analysis Phase consists of describing the "as is", the "to be" and a gap analysis. What is done in each of these parts of analysis? Why is each part important to the enterprise system implementation?

3. How is traditional business process reengineering related to enterprise system implementation?

4. What are the important decisions and deliverables associated with the first 3 phases of enterprise system implementation? How do you think they are used in the remaining phases of implementation?

References

Corbitt, Gail, Ron Noman, and Mark Butler. "Assessing Proximity to Fruition: A Case Study of Phases in CASE Technology Transfer." In D. E. Cooke (ed.), *Impact of CASE Technology on Software Process,* Vol. I. World Scientific Publishing Company, Spring 1994.

"Benchmark Implementations: Chevron Corporation SAP R/3 Implementation Study."
Cambridge, Mass.: Benchmarking Partners, 1997.

Chapter 10

Realizing and Operating Enterprise Systems

By the time [the Leaning Tower of Pisa] was 10% built, everyone knew it would be a total disaster. But the investment was so big they felt compelled to go on. — Ken Iverson

Once the detailed planning, analysis, and configuration decisions have been made, it is time to set up the enterprise system to support the business environment. This phase is called realization because this is where the requirements become a reality for the system and its organizational environment. During the realization phase of an implementation project, the requirements defined in the analysis and process design phases are configured and tested at a functional level. The development system is configured, tested, and validated, and it becomes ready for integrated testing. Many of the interfaces, conversion programs, special report programs,

---

OBJECTIVES

♦ Introduce the realization phase

♦ Understand the final phases of an implementation project

♦ Examine go live and support issues

---

and enhancements are designed and tested in the development environment, and plans are made for the systems test and go live.

Realizing the Enterprise System

Realizing the system within the organization is a time-consuming phase that has been planned for well in advance. The generic activities that can take place in this phase include installation of hardware and software; actual execution of the configuration decisions made in the analysis phase; determination of interfaces to legacy systems that are not replaced by the enterprise system in this implementation cycle; enhancements to the system, including at a minimum reports, forms, and screen layouts; major modifications to the system, including coding new programs, making modifications to existing programs and/or bolting on add-on applications to the enterprise system; converting data from the legacy systems; testing everything; and culminating in user acceptance. Although the list of activities is formulated primarily from the perspective of the business process team, to some extent each of these generic activities involves some level of participation by the technical team responsible for systems administration and by the change management team responsible for getting the user community ready to use the "go live" system.

Installation

The primary activities of the technical team during the realization phase revolve around installing and managing the system's landscape. Chapter Seven introduced the concept of change transport, where system enhancements and changes were isolated in development and then testing systems before being moved into a live production environment. Landscape is the term for this set of independent systems that are used to develop, configure, test, and operate an enterprise system.

A system landscape can be installed on one machine or server, or it can be spread out over multiple servers. Landscape does not refer to the total system topology, which, for a large organization, may include hundreds of servers spread across many regions of the country or world. Instead, landscape defines how data and application-specific changes are propagated from independent development, test, and production environments. Landscape designs are described according to its corresponding number of

Number of Tiers	Advantages	Disadvantages
One	Minimal hardware resources; Fewer administrative requirements.	Development can immediately affect production environment. No testing environment for global settings. Production performance can affect rest of system users. Upgrades with testing not possible.
Two (Production split from Development and Test)	Production data are secure from programmers. Performance of production users does not adversely affect developers. Lower resource cost than three- or four-tiered systems.	Development and testing are still done in same system. Changes in development can adversely affect test environment.
Three (Production, Test, and Development)	Production data are secure. Performance of development and test environments are not adversely affected. Test environment can be kept pure (mirrors production or "to be" production).	Hardware resources increase. More systems administrative functions.
Four (Production, Pre-Production, Test, Development)	Same as three plus: Full data loads and interfaces are tested prior to go live. Creates real training environment.	Even more hardware resources required. More systems administration.

TABLE 10-1. Advantages and disadvantages of alternative system landscapes.

tiers (not to be confused with client-server tiers). Each design has advantages and disadvantages; these are summarized in Table 10-1.

A single-tiered landscape means that development, testing, and production are all done on one database server. In SAP's R/3, this is achieved by having separate clients for development and configuration, testing, and production. An R/3 client is a structural component or the highest level in the organization's structure where separate data can reside. One client can have many companies within it. Obviously, the biggest advantage of a single tier landscape is the savings in hardware and the system's administration tasks. The risks are high, however, that a change in the development part of the database can contaminate the production and test "parts" of the database. The chance of a programmer bringing the whole system down is fairly high.

The most common landscape in medium to large firms is the three-tiered landscape, differentiated by development, testing, and production. The development system is used to create custom changes in the data, programs, or configuration tables. The changes are then migrated to the test environment where functional and integrated tests can take place. If an error is found, the changes are made in the development system and the changes are migrated back to the test environment for retesting. When the changes pass the integrated test, they are passed to the production environment.

In some cases, companies use a four-tiered landscape where an extra system is used for full go-live testing. At Chevron this is called the staging system, and at HP the second level of testing is called the Move To Production (MTP) environment. (Note that at the writing of this book, HP was thinking about going to a three-tiered landscape and eliminating the MTP system in parts of the company.)

Regardless of the number of systems in the landscape, separate installations of hardware and software occur in each. In addition, the systems administration activities generally include development and execution of the backup strategy, daily monitoring procedures, security design and administration, print capability, and network administration. Other system administration tasks include some configuration tasks that also need to be tested and be made ready for the production environment. For example, the system used for change control and transporting the configuration data from development to test needs to be configured and tested.

For each tier in the landscape, then, hardware needs to be installed, configured, and networked. The development system is used as a place to practice the needed processes and procedures that are required for a smooth efficient production system. The test system is used to test the business processes and procedures. In addition, volume and load testing are completed, and all operating procedures are formed, tested, and refined during this phase. In other words, this is a critical phase for understanding what it really takes to make the organization operational on the enterprise system platform.

Configuration

Configuration is a generic term that involves modifying the "plain vanilla" enterprise system to support the specific business processes, structure, and data requirements of a particular organization. In other words, configuration involves the unique set of combinations of company-specific parameters needed to operate the business on a day-to-day basis. Some objects that are set up and maintained by the system are industry specific, and others are specific to the organizational and operational structure of the company. Examples of industry-specific settings might include unique characteristics needed to support banking or insurance industry activities. However, every organization is unique and uses variations on many standard business processes. For example, some firms use centralized procurement functions to purchase goods from vendors, and others decentralize procurement activities. ERP packages are designed to support both types of procurement and can even be set up to do some purchases using the centralized model and others in a decentralized process.

Some configuration settings tell the enterprise system where to find the data for a process as well. For example, many companies start the enterprise system implementation with the financial accounting components of the system so that the system can generate consolidated balance sheets and profit and loss statements. In many cases, the human resources (HR) management function is not included in the initial implementation project. If HR is not an installed module, then the enterprise system needs to know that HR data for projects or production scheduling are not derived from HR tables in the database but come into the system from another source or are maintained manually.

Interfaces to Legacy Systems

In addition to configuration changes, numerous interfaces may be required to bring data in and out of the enterprise system. It is rare that a company uses the big bang approach and implements all components of the enterprise system at one time; a phased approach is far more common. This means that parts of each business process may still be maintained in a legacy system or a system that has been in place prior to use of an enterprise system. The larger and older the organization, the more numerous are the legacy systems that may require interfaces. Inbound interfaces are programs that convert incoming data into the format required by the enterprise system, and outbound interfaces take data from the enterprise system and put it into a format that can be used by legacy systems.

Since over a third of all enterprise systems are used to support external accounting in the first implementation project, let's use the example of having the accounting data in the enterprise system and the operational data in the legacy system. This means that sales orders, delivery notices or goods receipts, and even invoices are still generated by the company's legacy systems. Since the enterprise system is used for accounting purposes, invoices must be fed into it for purposes of maintaining a customer subledger (an account showing the invoices and payments for each customer), the accounts receivable for the company's balance sheet, and various other related general ledger accounts. A program needs to be written that can read the data from the legacy system and convert it into a format that can be read and maintained by the enterprise system.

To creating an interface for SAP's R/3, for example, a program is written that reads the exported invoice data from the legacy system, calls a data input program in R/3, converts each field in the inbound file to a corresponding field in R/3, and then has R/3 save the data in its database. Outbound examples include downloading data from the enterprise system to a report program, to a data warehouse for ad hoc reporting, or to some other system external to the enterprise system. All of these interfacing programs need to be specified by end users, written, and tested during the realization phase.

Customized Forms, Reports, and Screen Layouts

In addition to interfaces, an organization often wants to change the standard report programs, screen layouts, or forms used for external documents such as customer invoices, billing statements, and credit memos. Again, programs are specified, written, and tested to meet the special needs of a company. While direct changes to enterprise system programs are discouraged by most vendors, writing stand-alone programs is quite common because they are easier to identify and test during future upgrades and are easier to maintain during the normal course of developing, testing, and operating the enterprise system.

Data warehouses are commonly used for ad hoc reporting and creating reports to meet special unanticipated needs. However, many enterprise systems have internal report writer programs that allow companies to customize standard reports. So whether a company writes its own stand-alone programs or uses the enterprise system's report writer, time is needed to figure out what reports, screens, and forms are required. The programs then need to be designed, coded, and tested so that they will be ready when the enterprise system goes into production.

Authorizations

Another major area of realization is defining and testing the authorizations or levels of security needed for each potential end user. Typically, the business process roles are defined by user groups, and test IDs are created and used to test the configuration for each role. There are two aspects to security design: (1) the level of system security required to perform the actual tasks or procedures and (2) the accounting controls needed to perform each task. For example, within the area of accounts payable, the role of creating or maintaining vendor or supplier records is typically separated from that of entering invoices and approving the payment to vendors. Combining these into a single role violates basic accounting controls. For this reason, the functional specifications of each role are defined by a set of authorizations or levels of security needed to do each job.

The design of the security system starts with installation of the development system and continues even while the system is in production. The jobs and responsibilities of employees change, and the security system must be flexible enough to change with changing jobs and process descriptions. The system also needs to be designed so that troubleshooting problems are handled quickly and easily. When the system goes into production, people need to be able to perform their jobs and at the same time be prohibited from doing the jobs of others. Thus, creating the authorizations is the first step requiring extensive testing and validation throughout the implementation process.

Modifications, Add-ons, and Bolt-ons

As described in Chapter 9, there are two ways to bridge the gap between "as is" picture and "to be" picture: change the organization or change the system. Although preferred, it is sometimes too difficult or politically infeasible to change the organization or its processes to fit the enterprise system. In this case, the enterprise system will need to be modified or extended in some way.

Modifications are enhancements or changes to an enterprise system that are often designed and developed in-house. Typically these are written in a language that is compatible with the enterprise system. For example, modifications to SAP's R/3 are written in ABAP/4, its own programming environment.

Add-ons and bolt-ons are programs developed by software vendors to extend the capabilities of one or more ERP package. Ensuring that the enterprise system process and data requirements are compatible with the bolt-on package can be a formidable challenge. Some ERP vendors certify the compatibility of add-on and bolt-on products. The growing market for enterprise system bolt-on products is beginning to move from systems administration types of products such as backup, tuning, and enhanced security systems to include extended functionality to the enterprise system. For example, customer relationship management (CRM), supply chain management (SCM), and production optimizing systems are being "bolted" onto existing enterprise systems. The future sees no end to these types of programs that promise to extend the enterprise system into the world of electronic commerce applications.

Data Conversion

Converting data from existing or legacy systems into the new enterprise system occurs in every environment where computers have been used to run parts of the business. Although many companies do not enter historical information into the enterprise system, it is always necessary to enter the current data used by the company on a day-to-day basis. This is true for every component, module, and submodule that is within the scope of the implementation project. For example, if the accounting module is being used, current accounts and balances from the general ledger, accounts

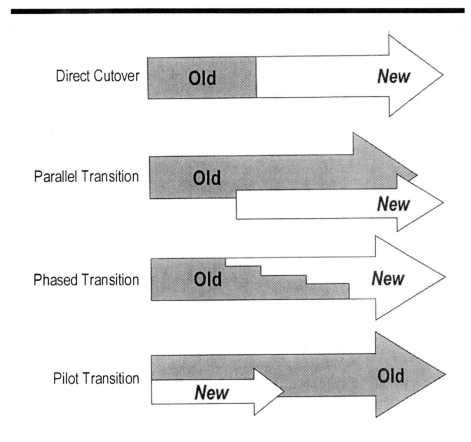

FIGURE 10-1. Alternative approaches to transition.

receivable, and accounts payable need to be converted from their legacy systems into the enterprise system.

Conversion programs are designed, written, and tested during the realization phase and are similar to interfaces. The biggest difference between data conversion programs and interfaces is that data conversions may be one-time uploads; as such, the ways to do conversion may be less varied than the ways to do interfacing programs. Some enterprise systems offer options for converting master data directly from spreadsheets and text files, whereas interfaces can become more complex depending on the source of the legacy data and the frequency of uploading or downloading. By definition, data conversion programs are always uploading data into the enterprise system.

Testing

At a minimum, two levels of testing must occur during the realization phase. First, each individual unit or function is tested on its own. This includes any data conversion programs, interfaces, authorizations, and enhancement or report programs. In addition to technological systems, unit or function testing includes organizational processes such as training materials and month-end close procedures.

Once all of the unit or function testing is complete, integration testing takes place. This means testing of the enterprise system as a whole. Integrated test plans are made and executed so that the whole system can be tested from end to end. The integration test in a "near-real" production environment is the final step before "go live."

It is fairly common that about half of the errors detected in this phase are security errors where end-user roles cannot perform some part of the whole process that they need to perform. The reason for this is that it is a common practice to err to the side of creating overly restrictive authorizations and then gradually easing off until each user or role has exactly the authorizations they require, and no more.

The reality is that moving from analysis to coding to function testing to integration testing rarely occurs in a sequential fashion. Although there are individual signoffs for the various steps in the implementation process, design, coding, and testing are iterative processes that are done in parallel within various process areas.

In some cases, a tier is added to the landscape as a staging environment that simulates the actual "go live" situation so that a full month-end close can take place. Full data loads are tested as part of the data conversion process, and interfaces are fully tested in the staging environment as well. These tests, along with volume, stress, backup, and recovery tests, give management some added confidence that the system is ready to support the actual organization.

Go Live and Support: Operating the Enterprise System

One of the last phases of enterprise system implementation is to put the production system in place for actual work. In many cases, this transition phase replaces literally hundreds of legacy systems and can be a significant change in the way the company does business. A direct cutover transition strategy is often used, especially in environments that use a staging platform. In a direct cutover transition the new enterprise system is turned "on," and the legacy systems are turned "off." Since the staging platform is used to do full conversions, integrated test, and so on, the parallel running of the systems is done prior to "go live." The staging environment makes the direct cutover transition strategy more feasible and removes the legacy systems so that the end users are forced to make the necessary business process or procedural changes.

Alternatives to the direct cutover transition strategy include parallel, phased, and pilot transition (Figure 10-1). In a parallel transition, the existing or legacy systems and the new enterprise system are operated concurrently for a previously specified period of time or until there is sufficient confidence that the new system is functioning properly. This is a low risk strategy that carries with it the burden of duplicating all data entry and possible confusion as to which system to depend on should differences arise. Phased transition, as discussed in Chapter 8, creates special problems in the case of enterprise systems, where integration across functional areas makes it difficult to divide the system into parts that can be implemented in phases. Pilot transition works well in a highly divisionalized organization, where an enterprise system can be implemented in an autonomous business unit before being deployed across the entire organization.

Other activities accomplished in the final phase of implementation include:

■ Quality assurance checks and evaluations.
■ Optimization and refinement of the production environment.
■ Follow-up training and assessment of end-user needs.
■ Refinement of systems administration procedures.
■ Project review.

As the enterprise system moves into postimplementation or maintenance, plans for upgrading the system from both a technical and a functional perspective are formulated. Generally, by the time the organization is in the "go live" phase, the ERP vendor has released more than one product revision, so the organization needs to evaluate the new release and essentially repeat the analysis, design, and testing phases for the new product's functionality.

The systems administration people move into daily monitoring of the operating system, networks, and database so that changes can be made to improve end-user performance or throughput. Metrics like buffer (memory) reads and writes, hits (reads and writes) on the database, and transaction code throughput are watched so that changes in how the computer's memory is configured can be made to improve performance. Tuning the database and memory buffers is a highly specialized field, and in large global platforms, there are usually two to three people who tune the database and buffers of the servers on a full-time basis. Knowledge about the end user's use of data is required in order to properly tune the database.

For example, a professional whose sole job is database tuning for IBM states that if a group of users is reading the same table over and over it may mean that only one or two rows of the table need to be loaded into the memory of the application server so that the reads of the database can be reduced. Loading one to two rows can save a lot of buffer space, and lack of specific knowledge of why the users are frequently using the same table may lead an inexperienced database tuner to load the whole table into the server's memory.

Summary

In this chapter we spent considerable time explaining the project activities that constitute the realization phase. This is often the most time-consuming phase, especially if the earlier phases have been hurried or done without major attention to detail. During this phase the configuration settings, data conversions, enhancements, and interfaces to legacy and bolt-on systems are being coded and tested.

Like other system development efforts, the testing phase is iterative with coding. As errors are found, changes are made and then retested. The final test is an integration test that is made prior to the final preparation to go live.

The final phases of enterprise system implementation include the final planning for go live and the actual go live and support phase. During the final phases the site is readied through training, data conversion, and final quality checks. The old legacy systems are turned off, and the organization is finally transitioned to the new enterprise system. At this point, the consultants and project team members exit the project, and the support and maintenance teams take over the running of the system.

Discussion Questions

1. Why is the realization phase the most time consuming? What are some things that can reduce or manage the time spent in this phase more effectively?

2. What is meant by system landscape?

3. Explain the relative advantages and disadvantages of a one-, two-, and three-tiered landscape.

4. What is the main advantage of a four-tiered over a three-tiered landscape? In what circumstances are the relative advantages worth the extra cost?

5. What is meant by configuration?

6. How does the configuration process nearly guarantee that no two implementations of a specific enterprise system such as SAP's R/3 version 4.6B are alike in different companies?

7. Configuration allows a company to customize an enterprise system to its specific business needs. Other than configuration, what can a company do to customize the system to meet its unique requirements?

8. Give some examples of inbound and outbound interfaces other than those already in the text.

9. In developing interfaces, why is it important to always write the interfacing program to go through the system itself and not write directly to the database?

10. People who do not understand the complexity of enterprise systems say things like, "just find the data elements you need from your in-house systems and write a program to write those to the appropriate tables in the database." Why is this not a workable idea within the context of an enterprise system?

11. What is meant by authorization within the context of enterprise systems? Why is it important?

12. From what is written in the text can you speculate as to some of the design criteria that may be important when designing security for enterprise system configuration and use within a company?

13. Bolt-on products for enterprise systems are becoming a major software market. Research the Internet and describe some of the most common bolt-on systems available.

14. How are data conversion programs different from interfacing and bolt-on programs? How are they the same?

15. Why is testing so important? Name some of the levels of testing that must be done in realizing an enterprise system implementation.

16. The final phase of the project prepares for "go live" and then supports the system after "go live." What are some of the issues that need to be addressed during the final planning phase of "go live?"

17. How is a staging environment for go live the final test? What is getting tested?

18. What does database tuning mean?

19. Why is it important that the project team disband after go live? Can you think of a situation when this might not be a good idea?

Chapter 11

People in Enterprise Systems

Men have become the tools of their tools. — Henry David Thoreau

The world of work has been going through a transformation during the past decade. In some ways the job picture is better than it's ever been, particularly for those with technical skills, but in other ways things are pretty grim. One thing we know for certain is that we are witnessing tremendous changes in the demand for labor, the type of work people perform, and the shape of the workplace itself.

This chapter provides an overview of the employment picture for those interested in enterprise systems. Primarily focused on implementation, jobs in the enterprise systems area are among the most highly paid and challenging in the industry. The chapter also discusses enterprise system roles that are not focused solely on implementation.

OBJECTIVES

♦ Examine employment surrounding enterprise systems implementation

♦ Look at nonimplementation-related jobs in enterprise systems

---

People in Implementation Projects

One of the first steps in an enterprise system implementation is to define the roles and responsibilities of the team. To a large extent, the scope of the project determines the people who will be involved in the project. In general, an implementation project is staffed either internally, by employees of the company itself, or externally, by employees of an IT vendor (e.g., to help with the hardware installation) or employees of a consulting partner. Table 11-1 provides a list of roles related to enterprise system implementation projects. Regardless of the source, however, the processes that the businesses use, the people who will use them, and the method of implementation all affect who is involved when, how, and where.

Internal People

Internal people involved with enterprise system implementation are commonly drawn from four areas within a company: (1) business process areas, (2) operations, (3) customer and/or vendor support, and (4) the IT department. For example, Hewlett-Packard just completed a reorganization of its financial services organization, and within each process area there are groups of people who are responsible for enterprise system implementation (configuration and setup), operations (getting the work done within the process area), support (helping with the day-to-day problems and issues that arise within any large data processing application), and process engineering (having responsibility for process improvement).

Business Process Engineers

Enterprise system implementation requires business process people for each of the functional modules that are within the project's scope. These people are responsible for implementing, documenting, and improving in-house processes used to get the work done that the business needs. These people typically have a background in the process area they represent, such as accounts receivable, human resource employee development, and materials procurement (buyers). The list is too long to enumerate here, but these are typically high-level people who have a good view of the overall process.

Operations

In addition to business process people, implementation efforts usually utilize people who are involved in the day-to-day operations within the process areas. These include people who are called "power users" as well as people who understand the day-to-day operational needs of the particular business area in question. For example, procurement experts may include people who are buyers and understand all the rules associated with buying or procuring a product from a vendor, as well as computer users who understand what the data requirements are for the legacy systems that support this business process.

In many large global companies, these day-to-day activities can include people (1) who research problems such as tracking down why a vendor did not get paid so that the support organization can have answers, (2) who understand geographic differences such as tracking the value added tax on incoming inventory, and (3) who interface with customer care or service organizations that deal with problem recording and/or tracking for business partners such as customers or vendors.

Support

The support areas typically handle problem or exception accounts for customers who have problems with order fulfillment, accounts receivable, or returned merchandise. Additional support areas are typically set up to deal with vendors who don't send merchandise in a timely fashion, who have problems with credit on account, or who have not received payment. The larger the organization, the more likely that support and service areas are decentralized by a specific process. This means that more areas need representation for the enterprise system implementation project.

IT Professionals

Another group of internal employees is the technical staff needed to support an enterprise system implementation. When a company's technical infrastructure is managed within the organization (i.e., the infrastructure has not been outsourced), the groups of IT professionals come from the following areas:

- Planning and modeling (strategic IT decision makers).

- Conversion and interfaces (people responsible for making sure the enterprise system "talks to" legacy applications either for getting the data into the system initially—conversion—or for exchanging data with other systems in the environment on a regular basis—interfaces).
- Network administration (people responsible for maintaining the network infrastructure).
- Database administration (a group whose responsibilities include database layout, tuning, backup, recovery, and monitoring database activity).
- Security administration (staff that assigns, maintains access to the system, and prohibits unwanted access).
- Life cycle management (a group that makes sure the platform stays current, large enough to handle growth, etc.).
- Technical writing (people who document the system requirements, procedures, etc., for the system's staff and sometimes even the process specifications).
- Enterprise application integration (a relatively new group of people who have some background in web-developed applications and are responsible for integrating the enterprise system into the B2B applications, such as procurement and customer shopping sites).

External People

Not only do implementation projects often involve several hundred people within an organization, but outside consultants are utilized heavily as well. Subject matter experts (SMEs) are used to help the organization learn about the enterprise system (how it works) and the best practices for implementing such a system. Consultants are also brought in to advise the business with regard to IT infrastructure issues on everything from what hardware to buy to how to tune the database and application servers. Consultants are often highly specialized in their areas of knowledge (e.g., order entry processes within R/3 or how to tune the application servers in Oracle). Such a high degree of specialization may seem extreme, but enterprise systems are extremely complex and the depth of knowledge required to understand how these systems functions in a variety of situations is not trivial.

Consultants from the "Big Five" accounting firms (Cap Gemini E&Y, Accenture, Price Waterhouse Coopers, KPMG, and Deloitte & Touche) have large enterprise system practices for different products such as SAP's R/3, PeopleSoft, and J. D. Edwards. Companies buy services from these firms primarily because they (1) understand businesses within industries, (2) are objective and independent from the software or hardware vendors, (3) have a wide range of people with different skill sets that they can deploy to any given project, and (4) typically offer good support. On the other hand, skills among consultants can vary widely, and, like many IT organizations, they often suffer from shortages of good people who can be used for any given project.

Smaller independent consulting companies also provide enterprise system consulting services. Companies like Sapient, Cambridge Technology Partners, EDS, CSC, and Siemens all offer services related to implementing and supporting various ERP products. Another source of consulting services is the hardware vendor like IBM, HP, Compaq, and Sun Microsystems. They offer services ranging from help in specifying and selecting hardware to business process implementation.

Some companies are choosing to completely outsource their enterprise system by contracting for services from an application service provider (ASP). In this case, the enterprise system is hosted externally with access provided to the company on a fee-for-service basis. However, the ASP-for-ERP business model is still unproven, and skeptics point out that many decisions must be made within the context of a business and therefore cannot be outsourced. For example, the process of verifying a preconfigured system against business requirements must still be done internally (IT-director 2000).

Project Roles

Perhaps the most critical job function with respect to enterprise system implementation is the *project manager*. Sometimes this person is from the consulting agency and is knowledgeable in the implementation methodology being deployed. Other times the person is internal to the business and works with the consulting partner on the methodology. In either case, the enterprise system implementation project requires a seasoned project manager who can manage the plan. This means the person can assign resources and determine the sequencing of tasks (serial or parallel) appropriately. The enterprise system project should not be viewed as an IT project managed by the IT department but rather from the business process side. Enterprise system implementation projects are more about people and process than they are about IT.

Along this same line is the need for change management personnel. Change management has two completely different aspects: (1) the managing of changes to the IT environment and (2) the managing of change in the people and processes. The IT change management professionals may initially come from the outside, so that the organization can get the "best of breed" when it comes to version control and developing a good process for allowing programming changes within the enterprise system environment. Although most companies keep these IT changes to a minimum, a process needs to be in place that allows for the review and management of proposed changes.

The more complex area of change management is that of converging enterprise system processes with the people who will use these processes. Site readiness, training, and other knowledge transfer issues, documentation of the procedural changes resulting from using the enterprise system, and other related areas need to be identified, planned, and managed throughout the life of the project. Again people can be hired from the outside to address these topics, but typically change management is a joint effort that starts out with consultants helping the in-house people. After the first roll-out (in a multiphased approach), the in-house group takes over this function and gets involved with the implementation from the beginning.

Among business process experts are people within the organization who are responsible for the business process or own the process or are in charge of engineering a global or standard process across parts of the organization. Examples include accounts receivable, sales organization, asset management, or procurement specialists. In addition, an organization may include subject matter experts or power users from any process area that is within scope for the implementation project. Internal auditors and testing experts are often assigned to project teams so that the new system can provide business controls and quality assurance.

In most cases, product experts come from the vendor or consulting partner in an implementation project. These experts specialize in a very narrowly defined area such as sales order processing, authorization, or cross-

Account Executive	Layout Developer
Application Consultant	Middleware Expert
Authorization Administrator	Network Administrator
Business Process Owner	Power User
Business Process Team Member	Process and Organization Consultant
Data Warehouse Consultant	Program Controls Developer
Data Architect	Program Controls Manager
Change Management Team Lead	Project Engineer
Consultant and Facilitator	Project Manager
Corporate Strategy Member	Reengineering Process Expert
Cross Application Developer	Regional Program Manager
Database Administrator	Subject Matter Expert
Development Manager	Supply Chain Architect
Documentation Developer	Systems Administrator
Help Desk Provider	Test Team Member
Internal Auditor	Training Developer
Internationalism Expert	Training Instructor
IT Expert	

TABLE 11-1. Examples of implementation roles.

application expertise such as currency or workflow. There may also be experts on data warehousing products, supply chain management, or web-based procurement bolt-on products if these are included in the project scope.

Technical experts have a wide diversity of skills in such areas as authorization, network administration, database administration, and overall systems administration. In addition, some people on the project team may be experts in data access, legacy systems, development or programming languages, interfacing, report writing tools, or help desk support. Middleware, web interface, and operating system experts may also be needed on the team.

Change management experts address the organization's ability to be ready for the changes brought about by the system. In addition, people are needed who can train end users, create and maintain documentation, write procedure manuals, and manage organizational changes brought about by system changes.

People in Nonimplementation Roles

For those who want to make a career out of enterprise systems and not work for a specific company on an enterprise system implementation project, three general directions are possible: (1) consulting, (2) development, or (3) service providing. The skill set required to succeed in each is different.

At the present time, consulting is by far the most common route for those business students with some enterprise system exposure and nontechnical business knowledge in a discipline other than information systems. For example, students with background in accounting or production management become proficient in their discipline and take one or two courses that use an enterprise system for exercises and in-class examples. These students are often hired by Professional Services Organizations (PSOs) such as Accenture, Cap Gemini E&Y, or Price Waterhouse Coopers. They become more proficient in the module or submodules that pertain to external accounting or production planning, for example, and then get assigned as consultants on an enterprise system implementation project. The types of jobs that these consultants do can range from product specialization required for configuration to training and implementation support.

These same consultant-type positions are available with the ERP vendors as well. For example, Oracle, PeopleSoft, and SAP all recruit at California State University (CSU), Chico, even though the product used there is SAP R/3. These students are popular with the competing vendors because, since the underlying concepts are the same for many of the ERP modules, the students can pick up the unique features offered by the vendor more quickly than someone who has not been exposed to enterprise systems at all.

A popular career route for information systems students or those university disciplines that are more computer-based is to find jobs doing development for the ERP vendors themselves or for a bolt-on product vendor. I2, Ariba, SAP Labs, and Oracle Development organizations are all employment candidates for those students who want to write code, do requirements analysis, or offer internal (systems administration) or external support services for these vendors. Development opportunities are also available within many companies that implement or use enterprise systems as well. Both IBM and Hewlett-Packard hire a number of CSU, Chico, students for in-house development and systems administration jobs.

The third common route for enterprise-systems-bound careers is with ASPs (Application Service Providers). This field is still in its infancy, but there are new companies that offer enterprise systems through the web. The attractiveness of this option is that the organization does not have to maintain the system or the staff to support it in-house. They buy the application and access for running their company from an external service provider. The downside to this approach is that much corporate data are sensitive and security is a major concern. It is also not clear how the customization works through an ASP. But with practice and time, ASPs are bound to become more popular and become a viable option for smaller organizations. This means the ASP will be competing for those with enterprise systems knowledge as well.

Summary

This chapter provided an overview of the employment picture for those interested in enterprise systems. The chapter began with a description of enterprise systems roles that are focused on implementation, which are among the most highly paid and challenging in the industry. The chapter also discussed enterprise system roles that are not focused solely on implementation.

Discussion Questions

1. What kinds of skills are companies most likely to look for external to the company?

2. What kinds of skill needs are most likely to be found internally?

3. Can you speculate on the relative importance of internal versus external job responsibilities to the overall success of an implementation project?

4. What is a business process engineer? What functions does this person perform before, during, and after implementation?

5. Why is it important to have operational and support people on the project team?

6. What are some of the IT jobs needed to support an enterprise system? How are these jobs the same or different from other types of IT jobs? (For example, how does a database administrator's job within an enterprise system environment differ from that within a non-ERP environment?)

7. If you had to choose consultants to work on an enterprise system implementation project, what qualities would you look for in them and why?

8. It has been said that you can tell how the company is approaching enterprise systems by the kinds of people that are on the project. What do you think this means? (*Hint:* Companies that approach enterprise system implementation as an IT project tend to underestimate the impact of the enterprise system on business process areas and in general have higher failure rates than companies that approach implementation as a business process reengineering project.)

9. Some speculate that within five years most major software "purchases" will be bought through Application Service Providers (ASPs). How does this prospect change the job market for business system's professionals?

10. What kinds of people or skills are needed for the change management roles that must be filled on the team?

11. Why does the project manager often have the most important role on the team?

12. Of the roles that are listed in the Table 11-1, which sound the most interesting to you? Why?

13. What kinds of jobs available within enterprise systems do not involve implementing a system?

14. As more and more companies implement enterprise systems and they become part of a company's infrastructure, like the network or database, how will the job market change for enterprise system "trained" students? Do you look forward to these changes? Why or why not?

15. How is the job market different for students who double major in IT and another business-related discipline such as accounting or marketing versus those students that are only IT majors?

References

SAP's R/3 Accelerated SAP Methodology (within the R/3 system version 4.6B)

"Is ERP Really ASPable?" *IT-Director*, June 12, 2000.

"Enabling the e-nterprise" *IT-Director*, June 12, 2000.

PART FOUR

Extending Enterprise Systems

*E*xtending the reach of enterprise systems is the theme of the fourth and final part of this book. Enterprise systems are extended upstream toward suppliers to create extended supply chain systems. By extending them downstream toward customers, enterprise systems integrate demand with supply and production data. And enterprise systems can be extended upward to support managers and executives.

Chapter 12

Integrating Backward: Extending the Supply Chain

A complex system that works is invariably found to have evolved from a simple system that worked. — John Gall

O ne major impact of enterprise systems has been the improvement of supply chain managment practices in many organizations. Prior to integrated enterprise systems, supply chain management was limited to focusing on internal flows of material. With the advent of enterprise systems, the focus of the supply chain and its management expanded from material flows to both material and information flows and from internal processes to both internal and external supply chain processes.

The chapter begins by defining supply chain management and extended supply chain management and then provides some background on traditional supply chain planning and execution. Key to the creation of extended supply chains are the alliances that are formed among enterprise partners, suppliers, and customers. The chapter discusses alliances and a prominent supply chain medium: vendor-managed inventory. The chapter also discusses other innovative supply chain models such as continuous replenishment and channel assembly. At the same time, managing traditional supply chain activities cannot be neglected for this is one of the greatest strengths of enterprise systems. Thus, the chapter concludes with a description of the basic activities of supply chain management such as procurement, distribution, and inventory management.

SCM and Extended SCM

Value is created in an enterprise through the production process and external logistics process of a good or service. In the production process, value is added through the effective management of the enterprise's internal supply chain. The external logistics process adds value through the efficient management of the supply chains external to the enterprise.

The typical supply chain involves the following:

1. Acquisition of raw materials, supplies, and services for the production process (procurement).
2. Conversion of those items into a good or service (production).
3. Internal distribution and storage of the final good or service (materials management).
4. Distribution to and ultimate consumption of the good or service by the customer (order fulfillment).

So applying the concept of internal and external supply chains, we find that the internal supply chain includes the production and materials management processes and that the external supply chain includes the procurement and order fulfillment processes (Handfield and Nichols, 1999).

But the supply chain is more than just flows of materials, supplies, and services; it also involves the flow of information, both logistical and financial. It is the efficient coordination of these two flows (physical and informational) that gives the enterprise a competitive advantage. An example is Wal-Mart and the process through which it replenishes some of its store shelf stock. When an item is sold at the cash register, that information is

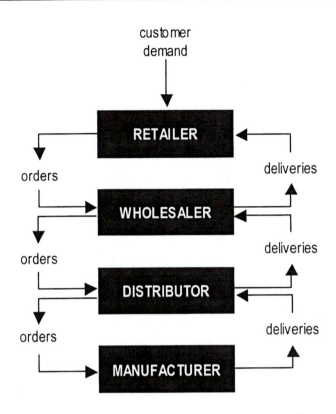

FIGURE 12-1. The supply chain.

relayed to the supplier to provide real-time information on sales of their products at Wal-Mart. The supplier then uses that information to determine what and how much stock to ship to Wal-Mart. The supplier of the product also uses the information to determine how much, when, and where to procure raw materials to produce the product they supply to Wal-Mart. So the flow of information impacts the flow of physical goods, and the coordination of these two flows leads to cost savings over the entire supply chain. This process is called *supply chain management.*

Supply chain management is the application of methodologies and techniques to integrate the processes of vendors, producers, distributors, and sellers. Through the application of these methodologies and techniques, the right product, at the right time, in the right quantity, and of the right quality is delivered to the right place. The goal and challenge of supply chain management is to achieve this at the lowest "total system" cost. Figure 12-1 provides a visual illustration of the supply chain.

As can be seen in this simple illustration of a supply chain, there are multiple relationships for every entity. It is the integration of these relationships that leads to the reduction in cost and improved quality of the overall process. However, several factors make this difficult (Simchi-Levi et al., 2000).

Each entity in the supply chain is operating within its own internal environment, which is likely different from that of many of the entities with which it is interfacing. For example, customers want the distributors and manufacturer's warehouses to have product available when they want it. In contrast, these distributors and manufacturer's warehouses want to maintain minimum inventory levels to reduce costs. This dilemma creates both internal and external conflicts as the different parties attempt to optimize their individual goals and objectives. To further complicate the matter, the manufacturer wants to produce the items at some economical lot size, often referred to as economic order quantity (EOQ). However, this requires accurate real-time demand information from distributors, warehouses, and the ultimate customer. In addition, the manufacturer is dependent on the suppliers having the necessary raw materials, supplies, and services available at the optimum quantity and time.

Further complicating this entire process is the fact that all of the individual entities in the supply chain are operating in very dynamic environments. Relationships change between supplier and manufacturer, manufacturer and distributor, and distributor and customer; the number of entities in a particular supply chain changes; the supply chain itself is always changing. These factors create an environment that makes management of the supply chain both more difficult and never ending.

Traditional Supply Chain Planning and Execution

As stated previously, there are both internal and external supply chains. Most organizations historically focused on the internal supply chains. This involved the processes of identifying and acquiring the resources needed for the organization to produce its good or service. The primary focus was on price, with a secondary focus on timing. The supply chain was viewed

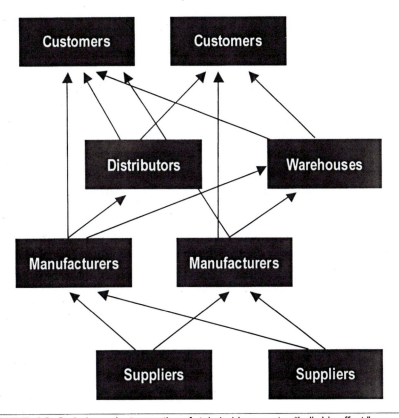

FIGURE 12-2. Independent operation of stakeholders creates "bullwhip effect."

as only a pipeline for the materials and services that the organization needed to operate.

The planning function in this traditional supply chain often involved frequent monitoring of raw material and component inventories to determine replacement quantities and frequencies. This monitoring was sometimes carried out using manual inventory control systems or a limited automated inventory control system.

The execution function of the supply chain was traditionally aligned with the planning function. When the manual system signaled the need for additional materials, the execution of this signaled requirement was initiated. This execution function was also a very manual process involving many process stakeholder inputs and approvals. The results of these manual planning and execution functions in the traditional supply chain were slow response, increased need for large safety stocks, and numerous non–value-added steps.

Another issue concerning traditional supply chain planning and execution was the fact that many stakeholders along the supply chain operated almost independently. Figure 12-2 illustrates this concept. As can be seen in this figure, each stakeholder in the supply chain depends on demand information from its downstream partner, who depends on demand information from its downstream partner, and so on. This creates a situation of high variability in demand data, even in environments with fairly constant demand. The phenomenon is called the bullwhip effect.

The retailer learns from the wholesaler that there is going to be a sales promotion discount on an item that the retailer stocks. Wanting to save money on the purchase of this item, the retailer decides to place a larger than normal order. The wholesaler receives larger than normal orders from several retailers and decides to increase its order from the distributor. The distributor in turn places a larger than normal order with the manufacturer. Seeing this increase in orders, the manufacturer concludes that the sales promotion has triggered an increase in demand for its product, and so it expands production. The problem is that once the sales promotion is over, the retailers may actually reduce their orders to balance inventory, sending a reverse wave down the supply chain. This causes the wholesaler to reduce orders because it does not want to have large amounts of inventory that is not moving. The distributor follows the same pattern, which leaves the manufacturer with expanded production, potentially significantly higher raw material inventories, and few, if any, orders. This entire process will repeat itself on a regular basis, especially if another sales discount is given to reduce inventories.

This traditional approach has changed with the growing use of computer systems to support supply chain management, the increased focus on the quality of materials being acquired, and the recognition that managing the supply chain was more than an operational activity. As management realized that supply chain management was a strategic function that could add value in the organization, the importance of this function increased tremendously. Currently, it is one of the hot topics within most organizations and receives focused attention from even top management.

Alliances and Vendor-Managed Inventory

The development of strategic alliances in the supply chain has a long history. Business enterprises have been establishing partnerships with their suppliers for thousands of years. The local baker, for example, would create a relationship with the local provider of grain or other ingredients it needed. Those alliances where based on location and need. Today strategic alliances are based on the desire to continuously improve the supply chain.

Jordan Lewis (Lewis, 1990) provides a structure for these alliances. He presents eight factors to be considered in developing these alliances.

1. Ways to Add Product Value: The alliance should address the gaps in your product offerings and supply chain, for example, partnering with an enterprise that focuses on repair or logistics.

2. Improved Market Access: The partnership could result in greater access to markets not previously tapped for both parties.

3. Strengthening Operations: The opportunity to learn from another organization arises.

4. How to Add Technological Strength: The partnership may help gain access to technology that is unavailable or underutilized. The opportunity to examine the partner's information system potential is also an important benefit.

5. Enhancing Strategic Growth: The opportunity to share resources and knowledge presents itself.

6. Organizational Reinforcement: Partnerships encourage shared learning opportunities.

7. Building Financial Strength: This involves the rewards gained through increased revenues, cost reduction through joint operations, and shared risks.

8. Look for Wider Synergies: Alliances can incorporate opportunities in the support areas of the enterprise.

These alliances also possess disadvantages and pose some problems. Enterprises can discover that the cultural differences between the organizations creates inefficiency. Organizations are very concerned about proprietary information and technology. For example, many high-tech manufacturing companies outsource a significant portion of their product line, especially mature products. The external manufacturers that they use are often the same ones used by their competition. So you could visit a Solectron plant and find that products are being made in the same plant for competitors. Control of the proprietary information by the alliance partner is critical in maintaining the firm's technological competitive advantage.

Alliances that involve outsourcing key components of the product can lead to overdependence on one or more suppliers and could result in the manufacturer handing control of the production process to a supplier. If the supplier is unable to meet schedule or technology specifications, the short-term effects may be serious and cause significant long-term consequences.

One type of strategic alliance that has been very successful in the retail industry and is gaining more application in manufacturing is vendor-managed inventory (VMI). A VMI program involves the vendor having visibility into the customer's inventory utilization. The vendor determines the replenishment policy needed to maintain the inventory at the agreed upon levels. Potential constraints placed on the vendor include storage capacity at the customer site, delivery schedules, and product control (perishables). Companies like Wal-Mart and Kmart have discovered the tremendous advantages of VMI, experiencing increases in inventory turnover rates of approximately 30 percent. Retailers have also reported increases in sales due to improved product availability.

A vendor-managed inventory program requires a good point of sale system (POS) or production control system to collect the data. In addition, the information system must be able to feed this real-time data to the vendor. Delays or inaccurate data feeds will create cascading problems in the supply chain. The transfer of data can occur using different technologies. One of the most common data transfer technologies is EDI (electronic data interchange). This data transfer method uses an industry standard to send different types of data through an electronic portal. Another method of transferring data is through a web interface. In this case, the vendor accesses the data through the customer's web site. This process is controlled through use of a login/password identifier. Some VMI partnerships allow the vendor direct access to the customer's information system. While this provides the most real-time information, it can create numerous security and software licensing problems.

Another issue in VMI concerns the point at which ownership of the inventory transfers to the customer. In some cases, this occurs upon delivery of the product; in other cases, ownership is transferred upon sale of the product. This type of arrangement is really consignment inventory. Another arrangement has the vendor owning the inventory until the final product is completed and moved to the finished goods storage area. In this situation, the vendor manages the inventory during the manufacturing process and is often paid when the finished good is shipped or placed in storage.

Implementation of any type of strategic alliance in the supply chain involves careful planning and monitoring. Issues such as data transfer, technology sharing, performance goals, confidentiality, organization culture, and financial commitments all need to be addressed thoroughly to improve the alliance's chance of success. An alliance failure may cost more than all the successes combined.

Supply Chain Models

Even though the basic supply chain concept is the same for all business organizations, application may differ markedly. We will call them supply chain models and present several of them here.

Integrated Make-to-Stock

The integrated make-to-stock supply chain model focuses on tracking customer demand in as real time as is feasible so that the production process can restock the finished goods inventory efficiently. This integration is often achieved through use of an information system that is fully integrated (an enterprise system). Through application of the enterprise system, the organization can receive real-time demand information that can be used to develop and modify production plans and schedules. This information is also integrated further down the supply chain to the procurement function, so that the modified production plans and schedules can be supported.

This integration allows the organization to assess any changes in demand and supply of the production process. Management can then react quickly to these changes.

Continuous Replenishment

The continuous replenishment model utilizes the strategic alliance concepts of vendor-managed inventory and just-in-time. The idea is to be constantly replenishing your inventory. However, the cost of this replenishment process must be extremely low, or this supply chain model will collapse. Very tight integration is needed between the order fulfillment process and the production process. Real-time information on demand changes is required in order for the production process to maintain the desired replenishment schedules and levels.

This model is most applicable to environments with stable demand patterns. Otherwise, the inventory levels of raw materials, components, and finished goods needed to support this model make the cost prohibitive.

Build-to-Order

Dell Computer is best known for its application of the build-to-order supply chain model. In this model, products are built after they are ordered and in a just-in-time fashion. The concept behind this model is to begin assembly of the customer's order almost immediately upon receipt of the order. This requires careful management of the component inventories and supply chain. A solution to this potential inventory problem is to utilize many common components so that the organization can take advantage of the "risk pooling" concept.

Risk pooling is most often applied to the aggregation of demand across several physical locations where inventory is maintained. It is used to assess the potential inventory reductions achieved through centralization of distribution centers. However, the risk-pooling concept can also be applied when we aggregate demand for a component across several product lines. Through use of risk pooling and a fast order management system, an organization can respond to orders quickly and maintain lower component inventory levels.

One of the primary benefits of this type of supply chain model is the perception that each customer is receiving a custom product. In addition, the customer is receiving it rapidly. This type of supply chain model supports the idea of mass customization.

Channel Assembly

A slight modification to the build-to-order supply chain model is channel assembly. In this model, the product is assembled as it moves through the distribution channel. This is accomplished through strategic alliances with third-party logistics (3PL) firms. Companies like Federal Express and UPS provide 3PL services to customers. These services sometimes involve physical assembly of a product at a 3PL facility or collection of finished components for delivery to the customer. For example, a computer company would have items such as the monitor shipped directly from its vendor to a 3PL facility. The customer's order would therefore only come together once all items were placed on a vehicle for delivery.

This supply chain model eliminates the non–value-added handling of components in the production process. The costs of shipping, handling, and storing a component that is ready for delivery to the final customer are avoided by having them move directly into the distribution system. However, order management is critical to making this model work. Because the 3PL firms do not want to carry large amounts of inventory in their facilities, careful coordination of all requirements is necessary.

Procurement

Managing organizational procurement can be an exteremely difficult task because of its highly cross-functional nature. Intergrated enterprise systems have significantly improved the procurement capabilities in firms where they have been deployed. In this section, we will examine the procurement process and catalog systems.

The Procurement Process

The purchasing process in a typical organization can be viewed as consisting of the eight steps shown in Figure 12-3 and described below.

Requirements Determination

This initial step of the process involves recognizing, defining, and describing the need. The need typically originates in the operating department or inventory control system. The purchasing department is notified through

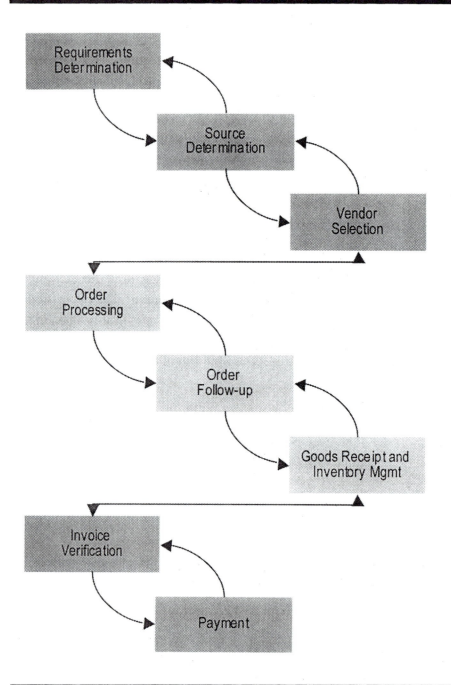

FIGURE 12-3. The procurement process.

one of two basic methods: (1) standard purchase requisition—internal document or (2) material requirements planning schedule.

Source Determination

In this step of the purchasing process, suppliers are identified, investigated, and qualified. The buyer begins the investigation of the market for potential sources of supply for the material or service required (often initiated by a purchase requisition). In contrast, the buyer may reference an existing supply source or sources that are already developed and evaluated. This is often called an approved vendor list.

Whether the source of supply is predetermined or identified through a search process, criteria are required to evaluate suppliers (quality, cost, past performance, etc.). In addition, vendor visits may be required in the purchase of large-value or critical supplies.

Vendor Selection

Once source determination has been completed and a list of qualified suppliers has been developed, a vendor needs to be selected. Competitive bidding and negotiations are the most commonly used methods. Competitive bidding is used when there is a large number of qualified suppliers, adequate time exists to issue bid request and receive bids, volume is high enough to justify, specifications are clear and not technically complex, and no preferred supplier exists.

Price is often a key component of the evaluation of competitive bids, but it is not the only one. Often quality, ability to meet delivery schedules, and technical abilities will be weighted as high or higher than the price.

Negotiation is used when early supplier involvement and a high level of product support are needed, when a long time period is required to design and produce the materials requested, when there are few or only one qualified suppliers, when material or service specifications are vague, or when performance factors are involved.

Over time, as a firm develops better supplier relationships, negotiation is the most commonly used method, with a focus on win-win situations for firm and supplier alike.

Order Processing

Once a supplier has been selected, a purchase order is prepared and issued. The purchase order (PO) contains information on the terms and conditions and is designed to give legal protection. It details critical information about the order: quantity, material or service specifications, quality requirements, price, delivery date, order date, method of shipment, ship-to address, and purchase order number.

A majority of companies utilize some form of electronic distribution of the purchase order and order acknowledgment (from the supplier). If they are not using electronic distribution, then seven to ten copies accompany the PO. These copies go to accounting, inventory control, the requesting department, the supplier, and so on. This manual process often takes days, if not weeks, to disseminate the information, thereby slowing the entire procurement process and adding no value. Procurement information systems and enterprise systems have eliminated many of the delays in the process.

Contracts, blanket purchase orders, and scheduling agreements are types of purchase orders that require different types of processing. If a firm consistently purchases a material from a single supplier over a long period of time, it makes more sense to establish a contract or blank PO. Orders are then released against the contract or blanket PO. A scheduling agreement is a contract with specified delivery dates for the material.

In addition, the purchase order determines whether the ordered material is placed in stock or consumed directly upon goods receipt.

Order Follow-Up

The order should be followed up to ensure delivery dates will be met. Follow-up also provides a firm with early information if there are going to be any problems with the order. Order follow-up is the responsibility of the purchasing department. It is also responsible for informing the rest of the interested parties about any changes in the purchase order (quantity and dates mainly).

Order follow-up may also include expediting, if the requesting party discovers that it may need the material sooner than originally planned.

Goods Receipt and Inventory Management

The goods receipt and inventory management step of the procurement process involves receiving the material, verifying that the correct material was received, sometimes inspecting the material, placing the material inventory, and managing the inventory.

From the viewpoint of procurement, the primary focus is on receiving the goods and verifying that the correct material was received. In the traditional procurement process, separate parties often performed this activity in two steps. The warehouse or stores operations would receive the goods and complete some form of receiving report. This report would then be forwarded to purchasing, which would check to see if what was received was what they ordered. If any discrepancies existed, an expediter in purchasing would be assigned to resolve them.

Through use of information systems, the receiving department can quickly determine whether the correct materials were received, based on access to an electronic copy of the purchase order. Receiving can therefore refuse delivery of a shipment if it does not match with the PO and if special shipment conditions are not included. Special shipment conditions include partial delivery, allowable material substitution, and samples.

Invoice Verification

An invoice is a request for payment normally issued by a vendor. The invoice verification process usually involves one of the following methods:

- Invoices based on purchase orders (three-part verification). All the items of a purchase order can be settled together, regardless of whether an item has been received in several partial deliveries. All the deliveries are totaled and posted as one item.
- Invoices based on goods receipt (two- or three-part verification). Each individual goods receipt is invoiced separately. The purchase order may or may not be referenced. It can be used for contracts and scheduling agreements.
- Invoices without an order reference. This normally requires a significant amount of manual effort in purchasing and accounting to determine where to post the invoice. Invoices of this type should be processed through the requesting department.

Some vendors can eliminate the invoice verification process altogether by instituting "evaluated receipt settlement." Evaluated receipt settlement allows one to settle goods receipts without receiving an invoice. Information is taken from the PO (price, taxes, payment terms, etc.) and goods receipt (quantity), and the information system creates an internal invoice. The advantages of this method are: (1) reduction of time in the payment cycle, (2) elimination of expediting of quantity and price discrepancies, and (3) reduction in data entry errors.

Payment

The final step of the procurement process is payment of the vendor. This function is normally performed in accounts payable, where all records of PO, goods receipts, and invoices are kept. In a traditional system, a payment request is processed after completion of successful invoice verification. This process can take days, weeks, or months depending on the approvals needed for payment.

Also included in the payment step are how a vendor wants to be paid and any payment discounts. This information is often included in a vendor master data file. The use of information systems allows much of this task to be performed automatically upon entering the vendor invoice. Many information systems will keep track of the discount terms and process payments to take advantage of them.

Catalog Systems

Another facet of the procurement system is the use of catalogs or catalog systems. These are often used in the purchase of supplies, often called MRO (maintenance, repair, and operations) inventory. In the past, this may have required the buyer to sift through a large number of supplier catalogs when selecting a source for the material. As a result, the buyer would often rely on a few selected suppliers for the materials, without assessing cost or delivery schedules.

With the development of online catalogs, the buyer can now search for materials more efficiently. However, the buyer is still focusing on one supplier at a time. Recently, software has been developed that allows the buyer to simultaneously search online catalogs of multiple suppliers. One of the leading software companies in this area is Ariba (Ariba, 2000).

The leading catalog systems are fully automated procurement systems. They not only assist the buyer in identifying sources for a particular material, but they also automate the entire procurement process from requisition to payment. The features and benefits of these software systems, according to Ariba, include the following:

- Buyers can more easily develop relationships with preferred suppliers. This will result in greater savings and win-win opportunities for both buyers and suppliers.
- The software provides greater global visibility to assist in identifying strategic sourcing alliances.
- The systems reduce and eliminate the use of nonstrategic, local, or one-off suppliers.
- The systems provide the capability to identify, control, and potentially eliminate off-contract and maverick purchasing.
- Procurement automation through use of the software will reduce cycle times and increase buyer productivity.
- Cycle time reductions will lead to across-the-board reductions in business process costs.
- Buyer productivity improvements that reduce the amount of time spent dealing with routine transactions allow for time to focus on strategic tasks, such as sourcing and commodity management.
- Overall improved order management and order visibility reduces the costs of procurement errors and improves procurement efficiency.

Just-In-Time Delivery

The concept of having materials arrive just as they are required is not completely new. In the traditional supply chain this was called rush delivery and expediting. The growth of the overnight delivery system in the late 1970s and early 1980s actually covered up poor planning in many organizations. The potential to receive materials overnight allowed organizations to hide supply chain management problems but sometimes at a significant cost.

As organizations recognized the need to manage the entire supply chain cost effectively, just-in-time delivery referred more to the event of the material arriving using the most economical and effective transportation method. This might mean using overnight delivery or two-day delivery airfreight, or it might mean the material is traveling by ocean freighter from Asia to the United States. The concept in strategic supply chain management is to select the delivery method that meets the needs of the system.

Just-in-time delivery has enormous application in the delivery of the product to the customer. This application of just-in-time delivery is discussed in the next chapter.

Summary

The traditional supply chain has changed significantly over the last decade. It has gone from a set of business processes focused primarily on the internal flow of materials to an integrated interorganizational system involving everything from procurement of the basic raw materials to recycling the used finished product. Through use of enterprise systems, the focus of the supply chain has expanded from a material flow to both material and information flow. In addition, these new supply chains extend to both internal and external supply chain processes.

Innovative supply chain models include concepts such as vendor-managed inventory, strategic vendor alliances, channel assembly, and just-in-time delivery. Each of these new concepts attempts either to eliminate waste in the supply chain or add value through cycle time reduction. However, many of the basic supply chain process requirements remain the same. These process requirements involve basic activities such as procurement, distribution, and inventory management. Managing these basic supply chain activities is essential for an organization to optimize its complete supply chain.

Discussion Questions

1. Explain the differences between the traditional supply chain and the current supply chain management concept.

2. What is vendor-managed inventory (VMI)? Describe an application of VMI and the benefits achieved through this application.

3. What are the similarities and differences between the "build to order" and "channel assembly" supply chain models?

4. Describe the different types of invoice verification. How can this process be streamlined?

5. What are the benefits of catalog systems in procurement?

References

Ariba, *http://www.ariba.com.*

Handfield, R., and E. Nichols. *Introduction to Supply Chain Management.* Englewood Cliffs, N.J.: Prentice Hall, 1999.

Lewis, J. *Partnerships for Profit.* New York: Free Press, 1990.

Simchi-Levi, D., P. Kaminsky, and E. Simchi-Lev. *Designing and Managing the Supply Chain.* New York: Irwin McGraw-Hill, 2000.

Chapter 13

Integrating Forward: Meeting Demand and Managing Customers

In this age, which believes that there is a short cut to everything, the greatest lesson to be learned is that the most difficult way is, in the long run, the easiest. — Henry Miller

W hy do organizations pamper their customers? Certainly, customers are critical because they consume the outputs that organizations produce. But these days, customers are not just a source of product consumption and revenue generation. Nearly as valuable as the income they generate is the information they provide. Today's most forward-looking organizations are intently focused on their customers because they hold the information keys to the demand side of the supply-demand equations that drive production in modern enterprises. The more high-quality information that an organization has about demand for

OBJECTIVES

♦ Describe new business models for e-commerce

♦ Explain innovative approaches to distribution and online retailing

♦ Discuss customer relationship management and introduce customer experience management

its products and/or services, the better able it is to manage supply. Thus, extending the reach of enterprise systems forward toward customers is the natural and necessary condition for achieving a fully integrated supply chain.

The chapter begins with a discussion of changes to the relationship between organizations and their customers that have led to an increased focus on the creation of customer value. The latest trend, e-commerce, is explored in terms of the phases through which organizations progress as they attempt to develop and deploy e-commerce solutions. Next, the chapter describes innovation that has occurred in distribution, specifically in online retailing and Internet-enabled enterprise systems. One of the most important technologies to emerge in recent years, customer relationship management (CRM), is introduced and key elements of CRM strategy are discussed, including sales force automation, the role of information technologies, and the newest direction of customer experience management.

Changing Business Models

Traditionally, the customer side of the supply chain focused primarily on getting the product to the customer and providing some limited service after delivery. However, companies must now focus on the entire experience a customer has with them. Simchi-Levi et al. (2000) calls this new focus "customer value," which, as they define it, is broken down into the five dimensions shown in Table 13-1.

The first dimension, conformance to requirements, is the basic ability to offer customers what they want. The supply chain provides the product to the customers where and when they want the product. For products with highly stable demand patterns, this function is relatively simple. However, when dealing with products where demand patterns vary and are not accurately predictable, this is a significant supply chain management issue.

The lack of available product from one company will cause the customer to go to another company for the same product or consider possible product substitution opportunities. The overabundance of a product will result in large inventory costs that damage the company's profitability. In addition, lack of flexibility in the supply chain to respond to the changing customer

1. Conformance to requirements

2. Product selection

3. Price and brand

4. Value-added services

5. Relationships and experiences

TABLE 13-1. Dimensions of customer value per Simchi-Levi et al. (2000).

product requirements will also negatively impact the ability to conform to requirements.

The second dimension of customer value is product selection. The issue here is how to deal with the large number of potential product configurations and still have all of them available to the customer. Some products such as personal computers and furniture have a large number of options, styles, and colors. For example, a couch may come in 15 different styles and 50 different types and colors of fabrics. If a furniture retailer were to stock each combination, it would have 750 couches in inventory. This is not a practical solution to the problem, especially when considering the variation in demand for each combination.

Several strategies have been developed to address this problem. One approach is manufacturer-to-order or assemble-to-order; this is one of the more common approaches in the furniture industry. The customer is offered immediate delivery of a limited number of combinations from stock or future delivery of any of the other potential combinations. This leads to another strategy, which is to offer only a limited number of combinations, an option provided to the customer in the furniture example. Some personal computer manufacturers that sell through retail- and warehouse-type operations use this strategy.

Yet another strategy is to distribute the large number of product combinations throughout the supply chain and take advantage of the concept of risk pooling (discussed in the previous chapter). With this strategy, products can be placed in regional distribution centers and sent to retailers when requested. The primary issue here is who pays for this inventory-carrying cost, the retailer or the manufacturer? A logical solution is to have them share the costs of this part of the supply chain.

Pricing and branding are additional dimensions of customer value. The issue of pricing is a difficult one to address. Many times customers are looking for the right time to buy the product in order to minimize the price they pay. Nothing frustrates customers more than making a purchase and then finding out two weeks later that the item they purchased is now on sale for 30 percent less. This has created the approach used extensively by Wal-Mart: to offer everyday low prices. This approach reduces the customer's frustration level and prevents large inventory swings as customers stock up when the prices are low and delay purchases when they view the prices as too high. In addition, this approach reduces supply chain costs by leveling demand.

The other side of this dimension is branding. With the wide variety of products available, manufacturers need to make their product stand out. Increasing the customer's brand awareness achieves this distinction. However, the costs in the supply chain may increase as a company seeks to maintain high product availability in order to avoid lost sales. So the customer value dimension of pricing and branding represent two sides of the same coin that must be balanced.

The fourth customer value dimension, value-added services, is a way of differentiating one company's supply chain from another. Suppliers are willing to offer services that provide customers greater supply chain efficiencies through improved information integration between the supplier and customer. For example, NUMMI has the seats for its vehicles delivered by the supplier in the exact order of the production requirements for the seats. This requires the supplier to have access to NUMMI's production plans so that blue fabric seats with leather trim, for example, arrive at the seat install station when the vehicle arrives at that assembly station. The value-added services dimension significantly reduces both inventory and material-handling costs in the NUMMI supply chain.

The final customer value dimension is relationships and experiences. Here the information part of the supply chain is maximized. The supplier collects as much information as possible about its customers. This information is used to improve the relationship with those customers by providing solutions to other parts of the customer value equation. For example, the supplier may be able to identify potential cost savings through product and service combinations. The customer appreciates the supplier for pointing out ways of reducing costs, and so the relationship grows. The long-term purpose is to develop a close alliance or partnership with customers so that they always think of you first.

Addressing the five dimensions of customer value in the supply chain is critical if customers are going to want to be part of the supplier's supply chain. The supply chain management strategy of an organization will impact customer value. Developing effective partnerships between suppliers and customers requires the integration of their supply chains, including the information flows. Only through this integration can the supply chain management goals of the enterprise be realized.

New Rules for the New Game: e-Commerce

E-commerce is the hottest game in town right now. Companies are spending large amounts of money to get "online." People with e-commerce technology experience are in high demand and demanding large salaries and often a piece of the action. The dot.com stories of instant millionaires are fueling the fire, but the pile of failures is growing as fast, if not faster, than the pile of successes. How does one make sense of all this commotion? Let us first examine the different levels of e-commerce.

Steph Marchak (Marchak, 2000) describes what he calls the "six levels of e-commerce development" (see Table 13-2):

Level 1: Minimal Online Presence—This is the "corporate web site." An organization takes this first step because it feels it has to be on the "net." This is a low-risk step. The technology requirements for this level are very basic and easily obtainable. Small- and medium-size firms may wish to stay at this level for a long period of time, for varied reasons. The firm may not feel it has the technology infrastructure to do more than this. Or the firm may believe that it is too expensive to move to the next level. For others, there may be internal conflicts as to what should be the next step, so going slow appears to be the best alternative to upper management. However, in the long run the survival of the firm may depend on moving to the next level.

1. Minimal Online Presence

2. Online Catalog

3. Online Order Entry

4. Automated Value Chain

5. Market Site

6. Super Market Site

TABLE 13-2. Six levels of e-commerce development per Marchak (2000).

Level 2: Online Catalog—At this level the firm is often responding to requests from customers for more online information. The reasons for moving to this level include better customer service, a chance for increased revenues, a method to reduce costs of handling customer inquiries, and higher productivity. The amount of information on the firm's web site at this level expands to include detailed product and service information. This allows customers to view the product and service offerings of the firm before initiating the buying process. In addition, customers can locate after-sales support information quickly and more efficiently. The technology required for this level is not much greater than that at level 1. The biggest issue here is maintaining current and accurate information on the web site. The next step is to allow online ordering of products and services. However, if the firm does not have the information technology backbone to process online orders, it may remain stuck at level 2.

Level 3: Online Order Entry—This level allows the customer not only to view product and service information, but also to order those products and services online. Features included at this level are customer accounts, order tracking, shipping information, and return processing. The primary issue at this level is order fulfillment. Experiences of the past several years have shown that poor order fulfillment processes have resulted in very unhappy customers and increased costs to the firm. Firms have discovered that they need to integrate their online order fulfillment processes with their back-office information systems. This integration is critical if a firm is going to be able to provide real-time information to the customer on product availability, shipping status, and financial data. The time and cost of implementing the required back-office systems and integrating them with the online sales process can be significant. As a result, many firms may decide that level 3 is not for them. However, with the competition moving into this new "distribution channel," the firm may have no choice if it wants to survive.

Level 4: Automated Value Chain—The firm now has the online order entry process fully integrated with the enterprise system. Things are running as smoothly as one can expect until the next requirement surfaces. This requirement involves integrating with the external supply chain (the value chain). To continually reduce cycle times in the supply chain, real-time information needs to be shared with suppliers so they can more effectively support the supply chain. This requires integration across the entire supply chain. When an order is received online or offline, processes in other parts of the supply chain receive this real-time information so that these processes are updated. For example, an online order for a product signals manufacturing that the product needs to be scheduled for production. A signal then goes to purchasing that a production order has been created and raw materials are needed to support the production order. The next step is signaling the supplier that raw materials are needed. At this point, the supplier's information system takes over and potentially follows the same process. This process can be automated to whatever level the firm desires. However, initially top management needs to assure all parties that the process functions properly, it is secure (privacy), channel conflict can be managed (online versus offline systems), and the information is accurate and timely. This level represents a significant change to the organization. Some people will not be comfortable in this new organization. Management must be prepared to manage the change and not have the change manage the organization.

Level 5: Market Site—At this level, a third party has integrated the automated value chains of competitors. The customer can now view and compare products across a particular market. The value here is that customers don't have to spend all their time accessing multiple web sites for online ordering. However, the issue becomes one of how a firm can differentiate itself. The customer can now view the firm's products and services in direct comparison to other firms' products and services. Some of the challenges of developing and maintaining market sites include establishing a critical mass of competitors, convincing the customer that the information is objective (not biased towards one firm), and determining financial support for the market site (e.g., customer membership, transaction fee, or listing fee).

Level 6: Super Market Site—The super market site is one step beyond the market site in which related and unrelated products and services are also included on the site. The purpose of this is to provide the customer one-stop shopping. Amazon.com is an example of a super market site. The success of the super market site will depend on the customers' feeling that they are receiving a good deal and on the objectivity of the information.

Innovation in Distribution

Moving the product to the end customer (the retailer, another manufacturer, or consumer) is part of the distribution function of the supply chain. A variety of distribution strategies are available to the supply chain, including:

- Private Warehousing: warehouses owned by the producer that keeps stock and provides it when requested by the end customer. Often used in a supply chain strategy of having regional distribution centers.
- Retail Distribution Centers: similar to a supplier private warehouse but often owned by the customer in a retail operation.
- Public Warehouse: warehouses owned by a third party that keeps stock from a variety of manufacturers and distributes the stock to the end customer. It can be combined with logistic services. These firms are known as third-party logistics (3PL) operations.
- Direct Shipment: items are shipped directly to the end customer. This supply chain distribution strategy is used for make-to-order and assemble-to-order items. This strategy can also include many Internet and mail order companies.
- Cross-docking: a technique used extensively in the retail industry where the product arrives at an end customer's warehouse/distribution center and is quickly processed (often less than eight hours) and shipped to a retail store. This distribution strategy, made famous by Wal-Mart, allows

the retailer to combine products from a variety of suppliers and to make single full-load truck shipments to the stores.

In selecting a distribution strategy for a firm's supply chain, several factors must be taken into consideration: namely, stock levels, costs, lead times, and service levels.

Online Retailing

One of the most widely known uses of the Internet is online retailing. Although business to consumer (B2C) represents only 10 percent of the total e-business market, it is the one that gets a lot of attention. Almost everyone in America has heard of Amazon. However, many of these B2C online retailing businesses make little, if any, profits. The current trend appears to be the brick-and-mortar retailers moving online. This will create an interesting dynamic since the online retailing business is different in many aspects from the store in the mall. For example, many bookstores that sell books to customers both through the web and through retail stores do not allow a customer who purchased a book online to return it to their stores. The end result may be losing that customer from both.

The solution to this and other issues in online retailing is the development of an integrated supply chain strategy that allows access to information anywhere and anytime. This supply chain strategy for online retailing must focus on the order fulfillment process and integrating with the enterprise system. These issues and others are discussed in the next section.

Key Issues for e-Business

There are a large number of key issues in the e-business area at any given time ranging from transaction security to web site design. In the supply chain management area, some of the more important issues include order fulfillment, backend integration, and real-time inventory.

The issue of order fulfillment was in the spotlight during Christmas of 1999. Many customers were extremely unhappy that items they had ordered were not going to reach them in time to be "put under the tree." Instead, many received notices of back-ordered products or late shipment. The faster a company can process an order, the more likely that customer will order again. In addition, the accuracy of the order and order fulfillment schedules promised to the customer are just as important. Some companies spend billions on developing engaging web sites and marketing, but forget about the nuts and bolts of the operation until it is too late. The problems of Christmas 1999 have caused many online retailers to rethink their approach to order fulfillment. They are the lucky ones, for some of their peers won't have the opportunity to rethink this issue.

Backend integration of a company's e-business implementation to its enterprise system is critical for an efficient supply chain. "Some 85 percent of CIO respondents to a survey conducted by Collaborative Research pointed to backend integration as their greatest implementation challenge" (*CIO Magazine,* 1999). Companies struggle with integration of their enterprise systems into their e-business implementations. However, they learn that this integration is essential if the e-business initiative is going to be successful. When these systems are not integrated, customers cannot view real-time order status, product availability information, and account information. This lack of integration creates an environment of multiple databases rather than a single source of real-time, complete, and consistent customer and operational knowledge.

Another key issue in the e-business supply chain area is the ability to know and communicate real-time inventory information. Customers want to know if the item listed on your web site is available now or when it will be. There is nothing more frustrating than ordering an item with the expectation of receiving it in several days, but instead receiving an e-mail stating that the item is not available and your order has been canceled. This ability to display real-time inventory information is related to the second issue of backend integration. Without integrating your web site with a backend or enterprise system, your customers will never receive accurate inventory information.

One company, Streamline, an online grocery and household items retailer, checked inventory only after the order was placed (Von Hoffman, 2000). If the item was not in stock, an employee would select a substitute. Often these substitutes were not acceptable to the customer, and so the result was unhappy customers who would complain or leave, which ultimately cost Streamline money. The solution was to actually reserve product when the customers placed their orders. This was accomplished through building real-time links between the web site and the company's enterprise system (SAP R/3). The company used the functionality of the SAP R/3 system to link receiving, picking, and other warehouse functions with the inventory control system and SAP's online store module, which interfaces with order management, accounting, and inventory control. The result is satisfied customers who can trust the company when it says an item is in stock and when it will be delivered.

Internet-Enabled Enterprise Systems

The need to move the company's enterprise system to the web and information from the web to the enterprise system is critical. Unfortunately, the information from the backend enterprise system doesn't find its way into the web and vice versa. Often an organization ends up with a separate web and enterprise applications with no integration. Information that would allow the organization to manage the supply chain more effectively is not shared.

The rapid growth of the electronic marketplace has triggered the need to link an organization's internal and external systems. The establishment of these electronic marketplaces will generate enormous integration challenges. The lack of connecting systems both internally and externally could render these electronic marketplaces both inefficient and costly.

Companies are setting up web infrastructures to improve customer service, to reduce procurement costs, to build new sales channels, and to increase product information availability. The company then realizes that the new and compelling web application needs to integrate with an existing enterprise system application or, worse, legacy systems. This task of integrating the different applications falls on the IT department and its often-overtaxed resources.

The solution to this problem is the establishment of an IT strategy and vision. The question that must be asked and answered is, "Can we get information from anywhere in our company to anywhere in our supply chain?" (Slater, 2000). Often the answer to this question is absolutely no. The responsibility of IT management is to develop the strategy and vision for becoming this integrated enterprise. Slater (2000) states that this vision must incorporate the company's infrastructure and logical connectivity, plan for the future needs of application integration, and be able to handle unforeseen IT issues (e.g., mergers and acquisitions). The requirement is that one must be able to access data from anywhere at anytime in the supply chain.

Customer Relationship Management

The global marketplace and the growth of the Internet economy require that an organization have better understanding of customer requirements if it is going to keep them as customers. Through this expanded customer knowledge, the organization can serve customers much more efficiently. This is accomplished through a new concept and technology called customer relationship management (CRM).

CRM systems involve the collection and recall of large amounts of customer information. This information includes the basic customer name and contacts plus sales history, repair history, payment history, customer industry information, date of last sales contact, and any open issues with the customer. CRM involves the integration of all this customer information throughout the entire supply chain.

CRM attempts to address all of the customer touch points, such as face-to-face, Internet, or phone. The system allows company employees and the customer to collaborate on a variety of levels, such as product inquiry, contract information, past order history, product repair and service, and account details. For example, a customer calls and requests product information. The CRM system identifies the customer's number and routes the call immediately to the customer service person responsible for that customer. This customer service person can see the customer's sales history, warranty coverage, repair and billing history, and other documentation related to products sold to that customer. This information allows the customer service representative to provide better and faster service to the customer.

This information can also be shared real-time with the field sales staff. The field salesperson who lives on the road can now have real-time information on the customers they are calling on. If there are some open issues with that customer, the field salesperson can check on the status of the issues. He or she can also view the status of any open orders or service problems, the latest information on products, prices, and current information concerning the competition.

CRM systems can be connected to an organization's web site, thereby allowing customers to directly access their own data about open sales and repair orders. In addition, new product information can be pushed out to the customers for products they are currently selling or using.

Sales Force Automation

The purpose of Sales Force Automation (SFA) is to sell more with less. SFA is the integration of sales and marketing processes to generate a sale using less time and effort. SFA's goal is to efficiently and effectively provide customers the information they want throughout the entire sales channel.

Customers want the following:

1. Timely and precise information about orders.
2. Quick and reliable responses to all inquiries.
3. Ability to meet scheduled commitments on time.
4. Frequent contact and follow-through.

An SFA solution must satisfy these customer requirements while lowering costs. This cost reduction in sales can be achieved through a variety of methods.

■ Make fewer and more productive sales calls—because your sales staff has current, more pertinent, and useful information. This method will often result in increased customer retention.

■ Lower communication costs—through the use of electronic mail and web sites, customers and sales staffs are provided the most current information.

■ Lower paperwork costs—out-of-date paper reports are eliminated, and the cost of distributing them to staff and customers is reduced.

■ Eliminate redundant data entry—real-time systems allow for all current information to be immediately available across the supply chain.

■ Lower training costs—new sales staff members have immediate access to all customer information with one system. The learning curve for multiple information systems is eliminated. In addition, training materials can be delivered electronically, thus reducing travel time and lost productivity resulting from attendance at training sessions.

■ Reduce administrative costs—through the integration of administrative components of the salesperson's job, such as call reports and expense reports, into the system, the salesperson becomes more productive.

The SFA systems utilize several different technologies. Often they incorporate enterprise systems, wireless technology, Internet resources, and portable computing. These SFA systems have become a major component of many CRM systems.

The Role of Information Technology in CRM

The implementation of CRM requires information technology to play a key and necessary role. Information technology involves the use of databases, data marts, data warehouses, and data mining.

The role of information technology in CRM includes collecting the required customer data, maintaining this data, and providing tools to analyze and report the data.

Payne (2000) states that "a 5% point increase in customer retention yields a profit, in net present value terms, of between 20% and 125%." Although managers are aware that increasing customer retention improves profitability, that can't quantify it. This leads to poor strategies and decisions when it comes to customer acquisition and retention.

To increase customer retention and develop better customer acquisition strategies, an organization must gain and retain the following information: measurement of customer retention, identification of root causes of defection and related key service issues, the cost of acquisition, the number of new customers acquired, the profitability of retained customers, and the development of corrective action to improve retention (Payne, 2000).

Through information technology, organizations can improve the economics of customer acquisition, customer retention, and the lifetime value of retained customers. In the business-to-business context, an example of this would be sales force automation—creating an information-empowered sales force that increases the sophistication of customer management. This can dramatically improve sales force productivity and significantly enhance bonds with the customer.

In business-consumer organizations that deal with a large number of customers, a critical issue will be increasing the quality of customer contact through tools such as sophisticated call centers and electronic commerce.

Organizations will need to determine the appropriate customer management strategy and then develop the appropriate information technology platform to suit their requirements, now and in the future. This task may involve a creative blending of a range of information technology infrastructures starting with databases and then progressively moving toward data marts, enterprise data warehouses, and integrated CRM solutions using electronic commerce. It may also involve using approaches such as data mining, event-driven marketing, and channel optimization. The ultimate objective will be to identify opportunities for increased profitability through enhanced customer acquisition, improved customer retention, and targeted cross selling.

Customer Experience Management

Everyone knows that giving and receiving feedback is a very important part of any process; it is no different in the CRM. In order to determine whether an organization's CRM system is performing as desired, one of the critical pieces of information is the customer's view of the system and system output. Traditionally, telephone or mail surveys were one of the more common ways of gathering information on customer interactions. However, a new area of e-business applications has developed over the last several years called customer experience management (CEM).

CEM systems collect information through web-based and e-mail-based tools. The next part of a CEM system involves reporting the feedback results in a way that is interactive and that will allow data query and comparisons. Finally, the CEM system must provide continuous automated customer feedback to provide a complete picture of what the customer wants.

One of the leading suppliers of CEM software and systems is CustomerCast. Its software is based on the principle of providing "anytime, anywhere access to real-time, continuous customer feedback" (CustomerCast, 2000). The CustomerCast eCustomerSatisfaction system provides users with interactive customer feedback. Users access the feedback through private web sites, giving them real-time, continuous customer, partner, and employee feedback any time, anywhere (CustomerCast, 2000).

Summary

The process of getting the product or service to the customer has changed from a basic order fulfillment/delivery process to one involving management of the entire customer experience. This customer experience is an integral part of the information flow in the extended supply chain.

Another significant development in the customer side of the supply chain has been the recent growth of online sales. Companies have gone from a basic presence on the Internet to a fully operational online store, including real-time inventory, order tracking, and delivery status tracking. Some of the key issues here include integration with a backend or enterprise system, real-time inventory management, order fulfillment accuracy, and the ability to get information real-time anywhere in the supply chain.

The forward integration of the supply chain has created a need to have accurate and real-time information on customers. This is being addressed through a new concept and technology called customer relationship management (CRM). The application of CRM into the supply chain allows the organization to collect large amounts of customer information that can be used to improve relationships with these customers. Extension of the CRM concept into managing the customer experience has created information systems to collect real-time customer feedback on their experiences and to provide real-time statistical analysis of this information.

Discussion Questions

1. What are the five dimensions of customer value?

2. What are some of the critical issues involved in moving from an online order entry model to an automated value chain model?

3. How can the concept of cross docking add value to the supply chain?

4. Why is the integration of an enterprise system into an organization's e-business strategy so important?

5. How does sales force automation achieve efficiencies in the supply chain?

6. What role does information technology play in CRM?

7. How would you use a CEM system for an online retail store?

References

CIO Magazine. "The Internet Changes Everything." *http://www.cio.com/.* August 15, 1999.

CustomerCast. *http://www.customercast.com/.* September 12, 2000.

Marchak, S. "The Six Levels of E-Commerce Development." *www.dotcomadvisor.com.* August 23, 2000.

Payne, A. "Customer Relationship Management." *http://www.crmassist.com/.* August 29, 2000.

Simchi-Levi, D., P. Kaminsky, and E. Simchi-Levi. *Designing and Managing the Supply Chain.* New York: Irwin McGraw-Hill, 2000.

Slater, D., "The Whole Is More Than Its Parts." *CIO Magazine,* May 15, 2000.

Von Hoffman, C. "Ain't Nothing Like the Real Thing." *CIO Magazine,* September 1, 2000.

Chapter 14

Integrating Upward: Supporting Managers and Executives

Whenever you see a successful business, someone once made a courageous decision. — Peter Drucker

B y integrating its information systems, an organization gains enhanced visibility into its internal processes. This visibility allows managers and executives to make more informed and often better decisions. As enterprise systems are extended toward customers, suppliers, and other stakeholders, the horizon of managers and executives is extended to the entire supply chain. The ability to obtain real-time information on the status of external as well as internal operations greatly increases the positive decision-making potential across all levels of management.

After describing the supply chain context for managerial decision making, this chapter discusses

OBJECTIVES

♦ Describe supply chain context for decision making

♦ Discuss advanced software packages and data warehouses

♦ Discuss Internet technologies that extend the capabilities of managers

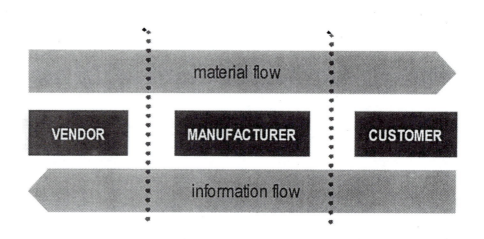

FIGURE 14-1. Flows in a supply chain system.

advanced software packages that allow managers to view and analyze real-time information that is tied to key performance indicators from the organization and its extended supply chain. The chapter then introduces data warehouses, which allow organizations to copy data generated by transaction processing systems and then create detailed analysis and reports on performance metrics for the organization. Finally, the chapter discusses the Internet and Internet technologies that show great promise in extending the capabilities of managers of integrated enterprises.

Supply Chain Information Systems

As mentioned previously, an organization's supply chain has two primary flows. Materials flow through the system predominantly from vendors to customers, and information flows mainly from customers to vendors. Figure 14-1 provides an illustration of this flow.

In an integrated supply chain information system, however, the information is flowing in both directions. Customers want to know the status of their orders, and vendors need to signal the shipment of material to the manufacturer. In addition, the manufacturer wants visibility into

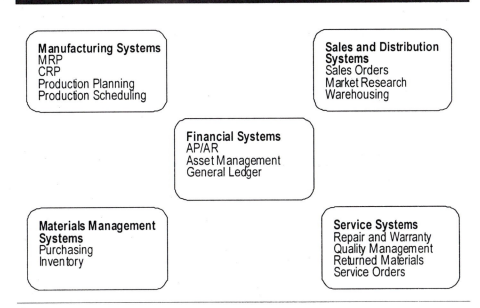

FIGURE 14-2. Traditional internal systems layout.

the information flows throughout the supply chain in order to make better decisions.

One of the critical issues in managing supply chain information is focusing on the integration points of the different stakeholders in the supply chain (vendor–manufacturer, manufacturer–customer). These integration points affect the organization's ability to properly manage the supply chain. The problem here is that many organizations cannot handle the integration of their internal systems, much less integrate their systems with an external system. In Figure 14-2, we see an example of an organization's traditional internal systems layout.

All of the systems displayed in Figure 14-2 were focused on one or two specific processes, and there was little, if any, interface between them. The development of enterprise systems and the improvement of supply chain management (SCM) systems have created an environment in which the organization can access information at any point in the supply chain. This new generation of information systems creates the opportunity for a single point of contact for all of the stakeholders, both internal and external.

Components of an SCIS

The goals of a supply chain information system are to collect, access, and analyze supply chain data (Simchi-Levi et al., 2000). In order to meet these goals, an SCIS needs to contain a portfolio of components (Simchi-Levi et al., 2000). These components include the following:

1. Procurement: creation and tracking of purchase orders, supplier selection and evaluation, maintenance of purchasing records and databases, and issue of bid request and evaluation of bids.

2. Demand Planning: a collaborative effort whereby different groups within the organization share information and analysis to create an overall demand forecast for the organization.

3. Logistics Network Design: determination of optimal factory and distribution center locations.

4. Capacity Planning: evaluation of the long-term and short-term capacity needs of the organization to meet customer demand.

5. Inventory Deployment: analysis of where and when to place inventory in the supply chain. The issue of pipeline inventory (inventory in transit) is critical here.

6. Material Requirements Planning (MRP): determination of component and materials requirements to support the production plan. This system uses bill-of-materials data, inventory data, and the production plan to determine when material needs to be produced or acquired.

7. Distribution Resource Planning (DRP): selection of the most cost-effective route and inventory movements based on customer demand, transportation and inventory costs, and facility (factory, warehouse, customer) locations.

8. Sales and Marketing Region Assignments: design of sales regions to maximize sales force efficiency and customer satisfaction.

9. Inventory Management: development of inventory policies and decisions based on the primary inventory cost factors of carrying costs, shortage costs, and ordering costs.

10. Production Deployment: in an organization with multiple manufacturing sites, the assignment of production requirements utilizing information concerning transportation, capacity, lead times, production costs, and demand.

11. Fleet Planning: selection of transportation mode and routes.

12. Available-To-Promise (ATP): ability to determine the availability of products or services when the customer places an order. This process takes into account vendor delivery information, production schedules, manufacturing lead times, and previously committed orders.

13. Production Scheduling: development of a feasible production schedule for a product given demand, production plan, capacity, and material and labor availability. The goal is often to minimize or eliminate late jobs (customer orders).

14. Workforce Scheduling: given the production schedule, development of a workforce schedule based on work rules and labor costs (overtime, shift bonuses, etc.).

Decision Analysis Tools

Decision analysis tools for supply chain management come in a variety of sizes and types. The leading provider of supply chain management tools is i2 Technologies (i2 Technologies, 2000). The SCM solution provided by i2 is called RHYTHM. RHYTHM integrates the different SCM processes that enable the exchange of information and movement of goods between suppliers and end customers, including manufacturers, distributors, retailers, and any other enterprise within the extended supply chain (i2 Technologies, 2000). The components of RHYTHM are:

■ Demand Planning: understanding and estimation of both short-term and long-term customer demand patterns. This information is fed directly to the supply planning process.

■ Supply Planning: optimal positioning of resources to meet demand. This process includes inventory planning, distribution planning, material allocation, and procurement interfaces.

■ Demand Fulfillment: provision of rapid, reliable, and accurate responses to orders. This process includes customer verification, order taking, ATP, order backlog management, and fulfillment of the order.

Another major player in the SCM decision analysis field is Manugistics (Manugistics, 2000). The Manugistics suite of products includes a wide variety of SCM components ranging from vendor-managed inventory to product configuration. Manugistics NetWORKS Solutions offer applications for the entire supply chain, including Demand Planning,

Supply Strategy, Order Commitment, Order Fulfillment, Supply Planning, Master Planning, Product Configuration, Transportation and Distribution Planning, Order Scheduling, Procurement Planning, Global ATP, and Vendor-Managed Inventory.

Other providers of SCM decision analysis software include SAP, Oracle, Logility, Symix, and Efinity (SCM Links, 2000). All of these companies offer either an entire suite of modules or a more focused set of solutions.

The similarities of all these products are found in each of their foundation components. These components are input data (direct or through a database or enterprise system), analytical tools, and presentation and reporting tools. The analytical tools include simulation, statistical analysis, queries, artificial intelligence, data mining, online analytical processing (OLAP), and mathematical models and algorithms (Simchi-Levi et al., 2000).

The presentation tools include the basic reports, charts, and figures. In addition, some of the systems include geographical information system (GIS) capabilities, which allow for graphical analysis of sales territories, transportation routes, and global views of supply movements.

Executive Information Systems

With all the decision-support and analysis tools for SCM systems that are now available, how does an executive decide which one is right for his or her organization? The critical issue here is the ability to quickly learn and utilize an executive information system (EIS). An overly complex system will result in either nonuse by the organization or the employment of analysts to run and print out reports for the upper management team. The problem with the latter alternative is that the information is not real time. How can this problem be overcome? Fortunately, several software companies have developed software that will push information to the executive's desktop. This push technology is essential if upper management is going to have real-time information concerning the supply chain.

One of the companies that is very active in the EIS area is SAP. Through the development of its Strategic Enterprise Management (SEM) package, it provides real-time strategic assessment connected to the real-time transaction engine of its SAP R/3 system (SAP, 2000). The SEM package helps the organization translate strategy into action. An organization that

GEOGRAPHIC INFORMATION SYSTEMS

A geographic information system (GIS) is a computer-based tool for mapping and analyzing things that exist and events that happen on earth. GIS technology integrates common database operations such as query and statistical analysis with the unique visualization and geographic analysis benefits offered by maps. These abilities distinguish GIS from other information systems and make it valuable to a wide range of public and private enterprises for explaining events, predicting outcomes, and planning strategies. (ESRI, 2000)

can execute strategy faster than the competition has a competitive advantage. A software package that allows senior management real-time visibility of key performance indicators can provide a tool to help obtain this competitive advantage. The EIS systems must be able to link transactions with strategy in a continuous fashion.

The components and functions of an EIS system may include the following:

- Balanced Scorecard: tracking and communication of financial and nonfinancial measures.
- Business Planning and Simulation: simulation and scenario analyses of markets, competitors, and internally.
- Business Editor: collection and categorization of current business information from multiple sources.
- Stakeholder Relationship Management: two-way communication of business information, including strategy, performance, and current initiatives.
- Performance Management: real-time monitoring and analysis of activity in the organization. This may include production data and order fulfillment data.

Data Warehouses and Enterprise Systems

As companies gain more experience with enterprise systems and SCM systems, one result is a large amount of transaction and planning data. Where to store and how to access this data becomes a strategic issue. If the data is left in the system of origin, then users must have access to all of the system they need to extract data from. The problem with this approach is that the user may wish to combine data from several systems to perform his or her analysis or to generate a report. The solution to this problem is the creation of a data warehouse.

On a periodic basis, information is copied from the system of data creation and ownership to a data warehouse where data from many systems are placed so that there is a single access point. Not all of the data from each of these systems needs to be copied to the data warehouse. Often only a selected portion of the data is copied based on user requirements. In addition, the data still exist in the system of origin.

One disadvantage of a data warehouse is that the data are not real time. Depending on how frequently data is copied into the data warehouse will affect the currency and value of the data. Recently, the concept of real-time data warehouses has surfaced (Johnson, 1999). The concept is to allow the user to view the data content real-time instead of through a "snapshot" that may be one or more weeks old. The challenge here is to be able to extract data from multiple sources in a variety of structured and unstructured formats. Some of the companies working on software to provide this capability are Vality, InfoRay, and MatrixOne (Johnson, 1999).

Another problem with some data warehouses is the large amount of information they contain, creating both hardware and software problems. The users of the data want to be able to access the data quickly. In addition, they want to be able to generate user-friendly reports that can be easily viewed, and they want the results to be easily evaluated. Therefore, the data warehouse must be so structured that it contains only the information required for analysis and reporting, and not every piece of data in the organization.

OLAP versus OLTP

In Chapter 5, we discussed the difference between online analytical processing (OLAP) and online transaction processing (OLTP) in terms of alternative designs of distributed information technologies that support them. Here, we discuss them in terms of their application to managerial decision-making. Recall that OLAP defines a class of methods that are developed to access and analyze data on a real-time basis. Whereas transaction processing usually depends on relational databases, and the OLAP methods require multidimensional views of business data.

OLTP focuses on transactions with a large number of users creating and retrieving data records, while OLAP applications require a higher view of the data for analysis. The OLAP database can be a data warehouse that is updated on a periodic basis from multiple systems.

The relational database approach is efficient when the goal is to retrieve a small number of records quickly. However, the process of retrieving a large number of records, summarizing, and rapidly analyzing the data does not represent a good application of the relational database. The OLAP technology using multidimensional databases is what is required for large data extraction, summary, and analysis.

OLTP applications often work with one real-time transaction data record at a time, whereas the OLAP applications work with historical aggregate data. This historical data requirement of OLAP applications means that the databases used with them must be able to deal with time-series data.

Data Mining

Data mining is a process that involves the extraction of important analytical information from a data warehouse in an effort to identify key success factors and business drivers within an organization. These tools automatically search through large amounts of data to detect trends and patterns.

Many companies have large databases or data warehouses that contain more information than could ever be analyzed by an individual or group of individuals. The role of the data mining tools is to dig into these massive data sources for clues to better business performance and decision. These data mining tools are sophisticated complex algorithms that take advantage of the enormous computing power of today's computers.

For data mining to be feasible, the technology required includes:

- Massive databases (data warehouses)
- Powerful multiprocessor computers
- Mathematical and statistical data mining algorithms

As organizations have moved from the single piece of transaction data to multidimensional data sources, the feasibility and usefulness of data mining techniques have matured. These techniques, integrated with the

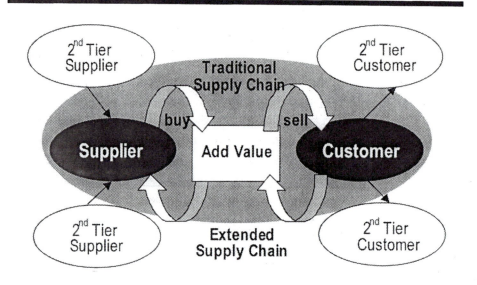

FIGURE 14-3. Extended supply chain relationships.

organization's enterprise system, have given the manager another tool in assessing the efficiency and effectiveness of the supply chain.

Interorganizational Systems

The traditional supply chain only included the suppliers through the customers. The extended supply chain moves down to the supplier's suppliers to the customer's customers. Figure 14-3 displays these relationships.

Fingar (2000) states that the Internet has made the extended supply chain a reality for many organizations. These organizations are now able to extend their supply chain technology and information systems to their suppliers and potentially their supplier's suppliers.

The extended supply chain information system allows the company to integrate with its suppliers, their suppliers, trading partners, customers, and their customers (Fingar, 2000). The integrated information systems share data from the point of sale to the available-to-promise inventory of the supplier's suppliers. Thus, competition moves from company against company to supply chain against supply chain.

The bottom-line payoff for this integrated supply chain is enormous, and all members of the supply chain benefit. However, if it were easy, everyone would be doing it. The information system requirements can be very complex. One of the biggest issues is communication between the systems. This is difficult enough within an organization, but add the complexity of multiple organizations of different sizes and information technology abilities and the difficulty can increase several orders of magnitude.

In order to give the integration an opportunity to work, many issues must be addressed, including:

1. Someone has to own the supply chain. A single point of responsibility is essential. This is usually the manufacturer, but a retailer may also drive the supply chain.

2. Security of information is critical and must be protected. This is because many supply chain members may also be members of a supply chain of the competition.

3. Companies must be willing to adopt communication standards. Outdated legacy systems will often derail the integration effort owing to the amount of data transfer interfacing programs required.

4. All members of the supply chain must share benefits, costs, and cost savings. No single supply chain stakeholder should receive the majority of the benefits or bear the major portion of the costs.

Summary

In a fully integrated supply chain, information flows both up and down the supply chain. The key here is to be able to access this information from any point in the supply chain. This is the role that information systems play in supply chain management.

Through integration of the components of the supply chain, supply chain stakeholders can view real-time information on the status of these component processes. However, this integration is not an easy matter. Many organizations have enough difficulty integrating the internal processes without also facing the complexity of integrating the external processes. This integration often requires connecting dissimilar information systems (enterprise or legacy systems), so that information can be shared across supply chain touch points (supplier–manufacturer, manufacturer–distributor, etc.).

Recently, developments in supply chain management software have included solutions to this integration requirement for the global enterprise. Providers of these solutions include i2, SAP, Oracle, Manugistics, and Logility. These software packages often include a standard set of analysis and presentation tools. More advanced software packages allow managers to view and analyze real-time information that is tied to key performance indicators of the supply chain.

Supply chain management software packages sometimes require the use of a data warehouse. These data warehouses allow organizations to copy data from many different systems (enterprise and legacy systems). This single location of data can then be used to generate analysis and reports on performance metrics for the organization's supply chain. However, this data is not real time, which can limit its usefulness to management.

The Internet has made the extended supply chain management a possibility. However, several issues involving security, communication standards, and ownership must be addressed before an information system can be implemented to support this extended supply chain.

Discussion Questions

1. What are some of the key issues in supply chain integration?

2. Who are some of the leaders in SCM software? What are the basic components of each of their packages?

3. Which components of a supply chain management information system offer integration points between stakeholders in the supply chain?

4. What role does EIS play in supply chain management?

5. What are some of the limitations of data warehouses?

6. Describe the differences between OLTP and OLAP. Provide examples of how each is used.

7. Which critical issues must be addressed to increase the likelihood that an interorganizational supply chain management information system will be successful?

References

Environmental Systems Research Institute, Inc. (ESRI). *http://www.esri.com/gisforeveryone/basics/*. September 15, 2000.

Fingar, P. "Transforming the Supply Chain." Logistics Management & Distribution Report, April 1, 2000.

i2 Technologies. *http://www.i2.com/*. September 15, 2000.

Johnson, A. "Viewing Data in Real-Time." *CIO Magazine*, December 1, 1999.

Manugistics. *http://www.manugistics.com/*. September 15, 2000.

SAP. *http://www.sap-ag.de/*. September 15, 2000.

Simchi-Levi, D., P. Kaminsky, and E. Simchi-Levi. *Designing and Managing the Supply Chain*. New York: Irwin McGraw-Hill, 2000.

Supply Chain Management Links. *http://sominfo.syr.edu/facstaff/xwang05/*. September 15, 2000.

Glossary

3PL Third-party logistics firms specialize in the provision of services related to the management and transportation of materials.

Add-ons Programs or systems that are designed to extend the capabilities of existing ERP products. May also be called bolt-ons.

Analysis and process design phase An implementation phase that involves analyzing the organization and its current processes, redesigning business processes as needed, and performing a gap analysis.

Application layer *See Business logic tier.*

Application servers Servers that implement the middle (or business logic) tier in a three-tier client-server architecture. In an enterprise system, an application server is responsible for running a specific group of applications, although, depending on the workload and other considerations, a unit of work may be routed to a different server. Also know as transaction or component servers.

Application Service Provider (ASP) Firm that hosts complex information systems applications for their clients on a contractual basis. ASPs represent a recent trend in outsourcing of information systems (including enterprise systems) by companies that do not have the resources or do not wish to take the risks associated with the latest technology. The attractiveness of this option is that the organization does not have to maintain the system or the staff to support it in-house, they rent it from an external firm that has developed strong capabilities with the technology.

ASP *See Application Service Provider.*

ATP *See Available-to-Promise.*

Available-to-Promise (ATP) The ability to determine the availability of products or services when the customer places an order. This process takes into account vendor delivery information, production schedules, manufacturing lead times, and previously committed orders.

B2B *See Business to Business.*

B2C *See Business to Consumer.*

Backend Common nickname for the data tier or a combination of the data tier and the business logic tier. Occasionally, backend is used to refer to enterprise systems or a collection of organizational information systems that are not as visible to those outside the organization. However, as enterprise systems are increasingly integrated across organizational boundaries, this usage is disappearing. *See also Data tier.*

Big Bang approach An enterprise system implementation approach whereby all the modules in this geography (all the targeted functionality) are implemented as one project.

Black box An object whose inner workings cannot be seen by the other objects that interact with it. As long as the object returns a consistent response to a message, no other object needs be concerned with how the object performs its tasks.

Blueprinting A top-down implementation strategy that involves looking at the processes within the enterprise system and finding the subset that best represents how the corporation wants to do business.

Bolt-ons Usually fully developed programs or systems designed to work with existing ERP systems. Also called add-ons.

Bottom-up data-driven approach An enterprise system implementation strategy designed to minimize the changes to the current business environment by mapping the existing data elements into the database of the enterprise system.

BPR *See Business Process Reengineering.*

Build-to-order A model in which products are built immediately after they are ordered and in a just-in-time fashion. The idea is to begin assembly of the customer's order upon receipt of the order.

Bullwhip effect An effect whereby each stakeholder in the supply chain depends on demand information from its downstream partner, who depends on demand information from its downstream partner, and so on. This creates a situation of high variability in demand data, even in environments with fairly constant demand.

Business case *See Project charter.*

Business logic tier Responsible for performing most of the processing that occurs in a client-server application except that which is specifically related to obtaining inputs and presenting outputs to the user (presentation tier) and storing and retrieving data from a database (data tier). Comprises all of the behind-the-scenes computation or calculation that is defined by business-specific rules rather than more general rules that apply to the management of data.

Business process Defined by Davenport as "A specific ordering of work activities across time and place, with a beginning, an end, and clearly identified inputs and output" (Davenport, 1993, p. 5). "A collection of activities that takes one or more kinds of input and creates an output that is of value to the customer" (Hammer and Champy, p. 35).

Business Process Reengineering (BPR) The redesign of business processes in an effort to reduce costs, increase efficiency and effectiveness, and improve quality.

BPR is characterized as radical rather than incremental in its approach to change and broad rather than narrow in its organization impact.

Business to Business (B2B) Term applied to that portion of electronic commerce conducted among businesses as opposed to B2C, which applies to e-commerce transactions between businesses and consumers. See also Business to consumer.

Business to Consumer (B2C) Term applied to that portion of electronic commerce conducted between businesses and end consumers as opposed to B2B, which applies to e-commerce transactions among businesses. B2C is also known as online retailing, e-tailing, web-based retailing. *See also Business to Business.*

Capacity planning The evaluation of the organization's long-term and short-term capacity to meet customer demand.

Cardinality A database term that defines how many of one type of entity can be related to another entity.

CEM *See Customer Experience Management.*

Change management Managing of changes to the IT environment and the change in the people and processes.

Channel assembly Assembly of the product as it moves through the distribution channel.

Chief Information Officer (CIO) The highest-ranking corporate officer in charge of information systems and technology.

CIO *See Chief Information Officer.*

Client Another term for the presentation tier within client-server systems.

Cluster A grouping of servers that perform similar work.

CODASYL Conference on Data Systems Languages, a joint U.S. government and industry standards-setting body.

COM *See Component Object Model.*

Common Object Request Broker Architecture (CORBA) Specification for distributed component applications that run on most operating system platforms. This specification is maintained by the Object Management Group (a consortium of about 800 companies) and competes with Microsoft's COM.

Component Object Model (COM) Specification for distributed component applications that run on Windows platforms. This Microsoft specification competes with CORBA.

Composite key A database key that is made up of more than one attribute.

Conceptual ERD A data model without any consideration of implementation details. *See also Entity Relationship Diagram.*

Configuration A generic term that involves modifying the "plain vanilla" enterprise system to support the specific business processes, structure, and data requirements of a particular organization.

Continuous replenishment Constant replenishment of retail inventory as items are sold. However, the cost of this replenishment process must be extremely low or this supply chain model collapses.

CORBA *See Common Object Request Broker Architecture.*

CRM *See Customer Relationship Management.*

Cross-docking Technique used extensively in the retail industry where a product arrives at a warehouse or distribution center and is quickly processed and shipped to a retail store.

Cross-functional process A process that spans multiple functional areas of the enterprise in a purely sequential fashion or involving reciprocal or simultaneous interactions between two or more functional areas.

Customer Experience Management (CEM) An information system that collects information through web-based and e-mail-based tools and reports the results in a way that allows data query and comparisons and is interactive. A CEM system relies on continuous automated customer feedback to create a complete picture of what the customer wants.

Customer Relationship Management (CRM) Technology that includes collecting the required customer data, maintaining this data, and providing tools to analyze and report the data. CRM systems involve the collection and recall of large amounts of customer information and the integration of all this customer information throughout the entire supply chain. CRM attempts to address all of the customer touch points, such as face-to-face, Internet, or phone. CRM allows an organization's employees and its customers to collaborate on a variety of levels, such as product inquiry, contract information, past order history, product repair and service, and account details.

Database Administrator (DBA) Technician responsible for the smooth operation of the DBMS. A DBA must make sure that the system operates in an efficient manner by "tuning" the database for optimal performance.

Data Definition Language (DDL) A language that defines all of the data and relationships within the database.

Data Manipulation Language (DML) A language that allows us to add, change, delete, and retrieve data from a database.

Data mining A process that involves the identification and removal of important analytical information from data warehouses. Data mining comprises a set of tools that automatically search through large amounts of data to detect trends and patterns.

Data tier The client-server tier that is responsible for data management, including the storage and retrieval of data from a range of possible sources. Commonly referred to as the *backend*, the data tier also provides backup and recovery services and transaction management.

Data warehouse A single accessible data storage point that contains data that are periodically culled from transactional systems for analytical purposes.

Database Management System (DBMS) An information system that organizes, manipulates, and retrieves data from one or more databases. A DBMS is arguably the single most necessary component in creating an enterprise system.

Database server Server that implements the data tier in a client-server architecture. They comprise the lowest layer in an enterprise system architecture. The database server usually incorporates a relational DBMS (e.g., Oracle, DB2, SQL Server).

DBA *See Database Administrator.*

DBMS *See Database Management System.*

DDL *See Data Definition Language.*

Deletion anomaly A situation that occurs when we inadvertently delete information that we need to maintain as a side effect of deleting other information.

Demand Planning A collaborative effort in which different groups within the organization share information and analysis to create an overall demand forecast for the organization.

Direct cutover A transition strategy that is often used especially in environments that use a staging platform. In a direct cutover situation, the new enterprise system is turned "on" immediately after the legacy systems are turned "off."

Distribution Resource Planning (DRP) Selection of the most cost-effective route and inventory movements based on customer demand, transportation and inventory costs, and facility (factory, warehouse, customer) locations.

DML *See Data Manipulation Language.*

DRP *See Distribution Resource Planning.*

EAI *See Enterprise Application Integration.*

Economic Order Quantity (EOQ) The economical lot size at which a manufacturer prefers to produce items. Requires accurate real-time demand information from distributors, warehouses, and the ultimate customer

EDI *See Electronic Data Interchange.*

EIS *See Executive Information System.*

Electronic Data Interchange (EDI) The exchange of standard business documents over computer networks.

Encapsulation The creation of an object's internal data structure and behavior so that they are self-governing and not visible to external objects. Thus, a change to a properly encapsulated object is invisible to other objects and totally self-contained.

ENIAC The first general-purpose electronic computer based on information technology (developed by John Eckert and John Mauchly).

Enterprise Application Integration (EAI) The process of integrating enterprise systems with applications such as procurement and customer shopping sites. EAI relies on a combination of web-based interfaces and component-based middleware to achieve integrated systems.

EAI *See Enterprise Application Integration.*

Enterprise Resource Planning (ERP) Complex software package commonly used to implement an enterprise information system. Major ERP vendors include SAP, PeopleSoft, Oracle, and J.D. Edwards.

Enterprise system An information system that integrates information from all functional areas of an organization with the goal of providing a more whole or complete information resource for the organization. The concept of enterprise systems can be traced backed to mid-1970's when database technology allowed, at least in principle, all applications to be supported by a common, centrally controlled database.

Enterprisewide information system *See enterprise system.*

Entity Relationship Diagram (ERD) A database diagram that is produced using a top-down modeling technique. ERDs focus on entities (tables) and relationships among entities in the database.

EOQ *See Economic Order Quantity.*

ERD *See Entity Relationship Diagram.*

ERP *See Enterprise Resource Planning.*

Evaluated receipt settlement Method that allows settlement of goods receipts without receiving an invoice. Information is taken from the PO (price, taxes, payment terms, etc.) and goods receipt (quantity), and the information system creates an internal invoice.

Executive information system (EIS) An information system that is used by executives and senior managers to assist them in unstructured decision making and communication.

Extranet An extension of an intranet to include entities outside the organization such as suppliers and customers.

See also Intranet.

Failover A mechanism for redirecting access or processing in the event the working resource fails.

Fat client A client that performs a great deal of processing activity within a client-server system. *See also Rich client.*

Fault tolerance The ability of a system to adapt to conditions that would ordinarily result in failure such as a power outage or surge. Most fault-tolerant systems incorporate redundancy and provide mechanisms for redirecting access or processing.

File server The simplest and most generic type of server in a client-server implementation.

First normal form A state within the normalization process of a database that requires that all tables are "flat" (i.e., each intersection of a row (record) and a column (attribute or field) must have only one value). *See also Normalization.*

Fleet planning The selection of transportation mode and routes.

Four-tier architecture Basis for most current web-enabled applications because presentation services are divided between the web server and the browser.

Front-end *See Presentation tier.*

Geographical Information System (GIS) A computer-based tool for mapping and analyzing things that exist and events that happen on earth.

GIS *See Geographical Information System.*

GL General Ledger.

Groupware Software for groups. Groupware is designed to support collaboration in a variety of scenarios ranging from face-to-face, synchronous meetings to dispersed, asynchronous activities.

HR Human Resources.

Information system A unique configuration of IT resources with organizational processes whereby the IT resources (and the information they provide) are applied to support specific organizational processes.

Information Technology (IT) A collection of generic technology resources—computer hardware, software, networks, databases—and the capability to combine them to support people engaged in meaningful organizational activities.

Initial implementation A first-time implementation, one that is performed where there is no organizational history of an enterprise system.

Initiation phase The phase in which the business case for the implementation is made, as well as major decisions about the project scope and implementation strategy. Also, this phase usually includes the selection of methodology, software and hardware vendors, and consulting partners.

Insertion anomaly An anomaly that occurs when information about two dissimilar data types is stored together as a single data element.

Integration According to Webster's Dictionary, "To make whole or complete by adding or bringing together parts." Information systems integration involves bringing together previously isolated information systems with the goal of providing a more whole or complete information resource for the organization. *See also Enterprise system.*

Internet The global network of computer networks.

Intranet An internal Internet or an organization-wide web.

Inventory deployment Analysis of where and when to place inventory in the supply chain. The issue of pipeline inventory (inventory in transit) is critical here.

IS *See Information system.*

Islands of automation Information systems that serve functional areas of the enterprise without regard to sharing the information that these systems generate and provide to business processes housed within that functional area.

IT *See Information Technology.*

Just-in-time delivery The event of the material arriving through use of the most economical and effective transportation mode to meet production needs at the precise time that these needs arise.

Key A single attribute or combination of attributes in a relation that will uniquely identify each row in that relation.

LAN *See Local Area Network.*

Large-Scale Integration (LSI) A level of integration in semiconductor technology that characterizes the fourth generation of computer technology. Using large-scale integration (LSI), engineers could fit hundreds of components onto a single chip.

Lean client A client that performs a minimal amount of processing activity within a client-server system. *See also Thin client.*

Legacy system Software and/or hardware system that has been with the organization a very long time and has not been upgraded to current standards.

Load balancing Balancing the processing workload across a network of computers, which often occurs between a server of one kind and a cluster of servers of another kind.

Local Area Network (LAN) A computer network that operates over a limited geographical distance (from one office to a few buildings) and is usually controlled by a single entity (an organization).

Logistics network design The determination of optimal factory and distribution center locations.

LSI *See Large-Scale Integration.*

Make-to-stock A supply chain model that focuses on producing goods and restocking the finished goods inventory based upon estimates of customer demand.

Material Requirements Planning (MRP) The determination of component and materials requirements to support the production plan. MRP uses bill-of-materials data, inventory data, and the production plan to determine when material needs to be produced or acquired.

Methodology The method or plan of action taken to accomplish a task.

Middle line The organizational part that comprises middle and lower-level managers who form the chain of authority between the operating core and strategic apex.

MIS Management Information System(s).

Modification anomaly An anomaly that occurs when the same piece of information is stored multiple times within the database.

Move to Production (MTP) The second level of testing on an enterprise system prior to transition.

MRO Maintenance, repair, and operations.

MRP *See Material Requirements Planning.*

MTP *See Move to Production.*

Multi-Valued Attribute (MVA) An attribute within a database that can take on multiple values within one record.

Mutual adjustment A method for coordinating tasks in a small organization through informal communication, simply by the workers talking with one another.

MVA *See Multi-Valued Attribute.*

Normal form Rules that allow the systematic separation of data into well-behaved tables that are free from anomalies and redundant data.

Normalization A bottom-up technique for arranging data elements into tables within a database in such a way as to prevent anomalies and redundant data.

OLAP *See Online Analytical Processing.*

OLTP *See Online Transaction Processing.*

Online Analytical Processing (OLAP) The ad hoc processing of historical data. *See also Online Transaction Processing.*

Online Transaction Processing (OLTP) The routine and immediate processing of transactional data. *See also Online Analytical Processing.*

Operating core The organizational part that consists of the workers who carry out the productive work of the organization.

Operation phase The phase of enterprise system implementation that involves ongoing efforts to monitor system performance and tune the system as appropriate. It also involves the continuing process of training employees on the enterprise system.

Organization A group of people engaged in some form of purposeful activity that extends over time. An organization has three components: people, processes, and structures.

Organizational process: *See Business process.*

Partial key dependency A second normal form violation that occurs in a database when any of the attributes in a table can be identified by a subset of the attributes that make up a composite key.

PC Personal computer.

Physical ERD Transformed conceptual ERD, which provides the implementation detail that supports the physical constraints of the database model being constructed. *See also Entity Relationship Diagram.*

Planning phase The phase of enterprise system implementation that is focused on setting up the project administration, determining the staffing arrangements, setting goals and objectives, acquiring resources, and establishing metrics for the implementation project.

PO Purchase Order.

POS Point of Sale.

Presentation tier The client-server tier that is responsible for providing a mechanism for a user to interact with an application.

Print server A server that coordinates network-printing activities and manages spooling and allocation of print jobs to various printer resources on a network.

Process *See Business process.*

Procurement The creation and tracking of purchase orders, supplier selection and evaluation, maintenance of purchasing records and databases, and issuance of bid request and evaluation of bids.

Project charter A high-level initial project-planning document. The project charter includes the business case for the enterprise system implementation.

Project manager A manager with proven project management experience. If selected internally, a project manager should come from a sufficiently high level within the organization to be able make decisions and changes quickly. If selected from a consulting firm, a project manager should be very knowledgeable in the implementation methodology being deployed. In either case, a project manager needs to have the full authority of top management to drive the project to completion on time.

Prototype A system that is designed for demonstration and evaluation purposes.

R&D Research and development.

RAID *See Redundant Array of Inexpensive Disks.*

Realization phase An enterprise system implementation phase that entails installing a base system, customizing to the organization, extending it if necessary, and testing the implementation.

Record A collection of related data fields that describe an entity in a database.

Redundant Array of Inexpensive Disks (RAID) A mass storage system that provides rapid access to data and several levels of fault tolerance.

Requirements determination The process of recognizing, defining, and describing the needs or requirements of a person, group, process, or system.

Response time The length of time from a user's request for information to the return of information to the user.

Rich client A client that performs a great deal of processing activity within a client-server system. *See also Fat client.*

Risk pooling A term that is applied to the aggregation of demand across several physical locations where inventory is maintained. It is used to assess the potential inventory reductions achieved through centralization of distribution centers. However, the risk-pooling concept can also be applied to the situation where demand for a component is aggregated across several product lines.

ROI Return on Investment.

Sales Force Automation (SFA) The integration of sales and marketing processes to generate a sale by using less time and effort. The focus of SFA is to efficiently and effectively provide customers the information they want throughout the entire sales channel.

SCM *See Supply Chain Management.*

SDLC *See System Development Life Cycle.*

Second normal form A state within the normalization process of a database that requires that all tables be in first normal form and contain no partial key dependencies. See also normalization.

SFA *See Sales Force Automation.*

SME *See Subject Matter Expert.*

Software engineering The discipline of application development, which is indicative of a highly technical and code-oriented process.

Source determination A step of the purchasing process in which suppliers are identified, investigated, and qualified.

SQL *See Structured Query Language.*

Strategic apex The organizational part that is made up of the top management team and is focused on achieving the organization's mission.

Structure The basis of coordination and control within organizations. It specifies how communication occurs and where power and authority are distributed. Structures may be formally articulated in an organization's procedures manuals, organization charts, and other places, but they also exist informally as is the case with unofficial social networks within an organization.

Structured Query Language (SQL) A standard language for manipulation of data and databases.

Subject Matter Expert (SME) A person with in-depth knowledge of a particular domain. SMEs are used to help the organization learn about the enterprise system (how it works) and the best practices for implementing such a system.

Supply Chain Management (SCM) The management of supplier, distributor, and customer logistics requirements in conjunction with a company's own production requirements.

Support staff Workers who provide a variety of types of support not directly related to production. These workers may be employed to support any level of the enterprise (e.g., legal counsel, bookkeeping, food services).

System (or Software) Development Life Cycle (SDLC) A generic methodology for software development that is often described as cyclical, consisting of a series of steps or phases that ultimately return to the starting point as new software is created or old software is renewed.

System landscape The set of independent systems that are required to develop, configure, test and operate the system. A system landscape can be installed on one machine or can be spread out over many servers.

TCP/IP *See Transmission Control Protocol/Internet Protocol.*

Technostructure The organizational part that consists of analysts such as engineers, accountants, planners who focus on standardization of tasks, outputs, and skills.

Thin client A client that performs a minimal amount of processing activity within a client-server system. *See also Lean client.*

Third normal form A state within the normalization process of a database that requires that all tables be in first second form and contain no transitive dependencies. *See also Normalization.*

Three-tier architecture Classic client-server architecture in which services are specialized and divided among three tiers: the presentation tier, the business logic tier, and the data tier.

Throughput The volume of transactions that can be processed in a given unit of time.

Transition phase A relatively short enterprise systemimplementation phase during which the organization's former information systems are replaced with the enterprise system. Transition approaches include direct cutover, parallel operation, phased transition, and pilot transition.

Transmission Control Protocol/Internet Protocol (TCP/IP) A collection of computer communication protocols that provide the underlying rules governing the transmission of data over the Internet.

Transport directory A physical location on a computer system that stores all change requests for the system landscape of an enterprise system.

Transport management A systematic approach to applying changes in an enterprise system whereby each change is applied to the systems from development to production in a sequential manner.

ULSI *See Ultra Large-Scale Integration.*

Ultra Large-Scale Integration (ULSI) A level of integration in semiconductor technology that characterizesthe fourth generation of computer technology. Using ultra large-scale integration, engineers squeeze millions of components onto a chip.

User interface An implementation feature of the presentation tier in a client-server system. Users interact through the user interface of a system by typing commands,clicking the mouse, etc.

Vendor Managed Inventory (VMI) A strategic alliance that involves a vendor having visibility into a customer's inventory utilization whereby the vendor determines the replenishment policy needed to maintain the inventory at the agreed upon levels.

Very Large-Scale Integration (VLSI) A level of integration in semiconductor technology that characterizesthe fourth generation of computer technology. Using very large-scale integration, engineers squeeze hundreds of thousands of components on a chip.

VLSI *See Very Large-Scale Integration.*

VMI *See Vendor Managed Inventory.*

WAN *See Wide Area Network.*

Wide Area Network (WAN) A computer network that operates over a broad geographical distance (from a few buildings to several countries) and is usually controlled by a single entity (an organization). *See also Local Area Network.*

Work Process Fundamental units of processing activity performed on an application server in an enterprise system. Each work process is generally associated with a unique task.

WWW World Wide Web.

Y2K Year 2000.

Index

Breinigsville, PA USA
06 August 2010
243079BV00013B/1/A